dream brave

"Wai Jia Tam's story of faith and perseverance has been a great blessing to witness. I love to see fresh generations of God's children pursuing total supernatural devotion to God's Kingdom, and her beautiful testimony is an example of so much that I always tried to preach and communicate. Love God, dream His dreams, and pursue them without fear—this is what she lives, and I invite you to listen to her with an open heart as she shares a precious example of all that this means in one family's wholly given life."

Heidi G. Baker, PhD, co-founder and executive chairman of the board, Iris Global

"We are all created to dream big, and *Dream Brave* will greatly inspire you to pursue your God-given dreams. Each chapter ends with reflection, activation, and prayer to empower you in your unique journey to dreaming big and dreaming bravely. This is a needed book in this hour."

Steve Backlund, Igniting Hope Ministries

"Dr. Wai Jia Tam has written a book worth reading, not just because it is packed full of truth, but because it is also an authentic expression of who she is. Every chapter records an encounter with God and a deep spiritual lesson learned about faith. Throughout the time I've had the privilege of knowing Wai Jia, she has been the personification of such courageous faith. She truly lives out the axiom that God did not call us to be safe, but He called us to be brave."

Pastor Benny Ho, senior pastor, Faith Community Church, Perth

"This is an inspiring and delightful book about having bold, brave dreams for God and seeing how He brings them to reality. Don't read this if you aren't open to be challenged and hear God's call."

J. John (Reverend Canon)

"If you've ever wondered whether the wild stories of Acts—featuring a God who answers fledgling faith—could be true today, read *Dream Brave*. From the very first story of being in a Malaysian

Buddhist temple and tentatively asking God if He was real, Dr. Tam invites us to listen and learn as she weaves together real stories, probing questions, Scriptural insight, and powerful testimonies of the God who still invites us to ask anything in His name."

Bronwyn Lea, pastor and author of *Beyond Awkward Side Hugs*

"Two words describe Dr. Wai Jia Tam, *others* and *obedience*. Her life is about serving others and walking in obedience to God. In this book, she is not just telling a story; she is inviting you into her story to experience adventure with God to fulfill His purpose."

Nicky S. Raiborde, lead pastor, International Family Church, South Carolina

"Wai Jia's stories are told with such color that they're going to pull you in. You're going to be right there with her, gazing at the faces, hearing the voices, feeling the emotions, and looking up at the towering impossibilities. When you see how God turned her impossibilities into possibilities, your heart will fill with confidence that God will do the same for you."

Bob Sorge, author of *Secrets of the Secret Place*

"If there is anyone who is qualified to write about dreaming brave, it is Wai Jia. She is a dreamer of dreams. But she does not just dream, she has the DNA of an 'Indiana Jones' who has seen many of those dreams come to pass. She is, in my estimation, one of the most colourful and adventurous people I know. She continues to amaze me with her stories of exploits with God, and I am certain there will be a Part Two to this book, because the adventure continues. I wholeheartedly recommend you read this book and dare to dream."

Reverend Yang Tuck Yoong, senior pastor, Cornerstone Community Church, Singapore; chairman, The Alliance of Pentecostal and Charismatic Churches in Singapore

dream brave

A Dare to Live by Faith When You Feel Too Small

Wai Jia Tam

Chosen
a division of Baker Publishing Group
Minneapolis, Minnesota

Published by Chosen Books
Minneapolis, Minnesota
www.chosenbooks.com

Chosen Books is a division of Baker Publishing Group, Grand Rapids, Michigan

Printed in the United States of America

ISBN 9780800763503 (paper)
ISBN 9780800772727 (casebound)
ISBN 9781493442393 (ebook)

Library of Congress Cataloging-in-Publication Control Number: 2023028501

The names and details of the people and situations described in this book have been changed or presented in composite form in order to ensure the privacy of those with whom the author has worked.

Published in association with Books & Such Literary Management, www.booksandsuch.com.

Baker Publishing Group publications use paper produced from sustainable forestry practices and post-consumer waste whenever possible.

24 25 26 27 28 29 30 7 6 5 4 3 2 1

To Cliff,
who inspires me to take bold risks for God,
and to my sweethearts, Sarah-Faith and Esther-Praise,
who sow faith and courage in me every day.

This book is for you,
for all those who long to
dream brave, and

for God,
who made it all
worthwhile.

CONTENTS

INTRODUCTION

DO YOU HAVE DREAMS in your heart that you long to fulfill? Yet a voice tells you that you can't, that those dreams are too big, too farfetched? How do you know if they're from God? What if they're simply mere whims?

The world's voices only confuse us more. They tell us, *Aim high!* and, *You can change the world!* So which of our dreams are from God, and which are those we need to let go? What are the dreams we need to die to, and which are those we need to abandon our all for?

The truth is that to believe in a dream requires not just vulnerability, hope, and courage, but also risk. It demands the brave acceptance of the possibility of failure. And to be *all in* without any sign of guaranteed victory is to take the biggest chance of all. To trust God even when the chances of success seem impossibly slim and pursuing a dream costs us something can often be the hardest thing to do.

This is where faith comes in. When we feel too small to discern God's dreams for our lives and inadequate to pursue them, faith believes He will guide us.

Amid the overwhelming, seemingly impossible dreams we have in our hearts, all God needs is for us to have faith as a mustard seed—that which is seemingly small but strong, resilient, and hopeful to grow into something of substance and sustenance in due time (Matthew 13:31–32). Because it is not the size of our faith that matters, but in whom we trust. Our little faith, when placed rightly in the hands of a big God, can grow to become an oak tree, sturdy and sure. Our little faith can move mountains (Matthew 17:20).

This is the foundation of *dreaming brave*, to take courage to pursue a dream, God's way, when we don't even know how.

Before we go on, let me share that I'm relieved God doesn't require better qualifications or high accolades from us. He doesn't want our shiny medals. After all, we can't change the world on our own, no matter how good we are. But we can give even our littlest dreams to a big God who can sow into them, grow them, anchor them on His cross, and make them fly—transform them into what I call kitedreams.[1] Without inviting His hand into our lives, none of our dreams will ever amount to more than what our human strength can muster. They'll only fall short of the glorious, God-sized adventures that tell of the extraordinary.

I want to encourage you, dear friend, that God has the power to bring your dreams of any size to fruition when they're according to His will and you follow Him in faith. I think you'll see that in the stories I have to tell.

In this book, let me take you on an adventure as we explore the Great Hall of Faith in Hebrews 11 and unpack faith through the sharing of twenty stories from my own experiences. My hope is that each chapter will bring to life an aspect of faith you have never seen or known. And I pray that after reading *Dream Brave*, you'll have the confidence and courage to apply faith as a powerful weapon to bring God's dreams for your life to pass and you'll dare to take the risks needed to follow through.

You see, once our dreams are anchored in faith, they gain clarity and momentum, growing into unstoppable callings. What might have started as a faint dream becomes a clarion call beckoning us to answer, compelling us to action. What started as a mustard seed will move mountains.

Lest we forget, God is not in the business of cause and effect; He deals in the miraculous. He's in the business of transforming five loaves and two fish into baskets full of leftovers, of turning water into wine. Filled with that assurance, will you toss aside any calculated backup plans you have for the dreams you know God has given you? Will you abide in Christ and entrust Him with your mustard-seed–sized faith?

Following each chapter in this book are

- prompts for reflection,
- proposed next steps for dreaming brave with faith,
- and a guided personal prayer.

I recommend using a notebook or journal (there is a PDF of one available at kitedreams.org/dreambrave) to record your reflections, your intent to take specific steps, and any prayers you wish to write out in your own words.

As you journey through this book, may God reveal to you that no dream is too big or small for Jesus. No matter how implausible those dreams might seem, no matter how small we feel, He is able. Anchored on the cross of Christ and buoyed by the Holy Spirit, our dreams—our kitedreams—can soar high when we dare to dream brave and live by faith.

1

when loved ones say no, hold on to faith

> Faith is the substance of things hoped for, the evidence of things not seen.
>
> —Hebrews 11:1

DURING MY FAMILY'S ANNUAL rite of passage visiting famous temples in Malaysia and having our fortunes told, I watched the throng of people queue up to receive their destinies typed onto little pink slips of paper. I nearly choked from the smell of incense. Kneeling on the hard prayer cushion, the sensation of pins and needles filled my legs.

As my eyes beheld the hundred-foot-long sleeping Buddha made of gold, I asked God, *Are you real?*

How I jolted upright when I heard words spoken to my spirit in a way I'd never experienced: *Yes, I am. But I'm not here. Find Me.* I rose to my feet, hands tingling, sure my life would never be the same.

When I picked up my first Bible just days later, I flipped to the book of Hebrews, and Hebrews 11:1 leapt into my heart: "Faith is the substance of things hoped for, the evidence of things not seen." *What a puzzling verse*, I thought. *How can something as unquantifiable as faith be as tangible as a substance or proof for "evidence of things not seen"?*

In Greek, the word for "substance" is *hupostasis*, meaning confidence or assurance, and some commentaries even suggest the sense of a "title-deed."[1] How mind-blowing it is to conceive that faith alone gives us the certainty of an unseen, eternal inheritance, that it's as real and powerful as a title deed that confers us the right of a heavenly heritage and legacy.

How can a seed of faith bring one hope when doors seem tightly closed? How can a whimsical idea combust into robust reality? Through an incident that changed my life, I learned all that can happen by a simple act of faith.

Persist in Prayer

At eighteen years of age, I had a little dream. But my pre-Christian and very Asian father immediately said no to it.

We were eating dinner at home when I casually asked if I could go to Nepal for a few weeks to help at a children's home. I might as well have said I wanted to migrate to Antarctica, because the silence that followed only thickened. I don't think my father quite knew how to respond.

"What?" he finally said.

Early in my life, my parents had already circumscribed my future. In Asian families, it's a standing joke that children are allowed only four aspirations—to be a doctor, a lawyer, an engineer, or an accountant, in that order of priority. I was seven years old the first time my dad asked me what I wanted to be when I grew up. With unparalleled confidence, I declared, "A painter." Year after year, my answer was the same, and every time my father challenged me—as though I were ten years older—until I eventually agreed that being a doctor was the noblest profession ever.

Once while on vacation in New Zealand, we stumbled upon an elderly street painter, his hands marred from years of toil. As if my father had perfectly orchestrated the scene for the conversation that would follow, the man smiled surreptitiously when he said to us, "It's a hard life. Painting is a passport to poverty."

Moved by the man's plight, my father bought a beautiful oil painting of the sea from him, then hung it on a wall in my bedroom. Whenever I asked to apply to art college, he'd say, "You can always be a doctor who paints but not vice versa." I would protest, and he would point to the painting, smile, and add, "Don't forget, painting is a passport to poverty."

Often, he would also say, "Work as hard as you can to be the best you can, so you can do as much good as you can for the world." I could see why he said that. As the eighth of nine children, he told of his family members "sleeping like potatoes" in a single room while growing up in a village in Kedah, Malaysia, with only yams and pineapples to eat. Once, hospitalized for being severely malnourished, he clung to life.

He loved recounting his past, sharing the miracle of his being sponsored to America for college and how he and my mother worked in pizza parlors and washed dishes in family restaurants to make ends meet. He talked of the winters being so cold he'd seek shelter in hotel lobbies only to have guards shoo him away because he looked so shabby.

"No matter how poor someone is," he always said, "treat them with dignity. Remember, Papa once struggled too."

A year after I was born in Malaysia, my father moved our family to Singapore, where he believed we would have a better future. Graduating from medical school, doctoring, and living a comfortable life were the markers of success he had planned for me. So imagine the shock he suffered when I asked to go to Nepal.

I remember the chortle that came after the "What?" before his face straightened. "Why?" He looked at me in bewilderment, a frown stretching across his tired face as I shared how I'd made a few calls to mission organizations, asking if any help was needed.

"But surely you can help people here," he said.

I love my father's capacious nature, something in his spirit that stretches. For even when he said no, even when I took him on long routes of negotiation, he never got angry. Much of it might have had to do with his having risen to meet the hardships of his childhood.

One night he told me, "You don't know anyone there. How can I trust someone I haven't met to look after you?" And on another night he said, "There are lots of schools with children with disabilities in Singapore who would be happy to have you as a volunteer." Night after night, we performed this dialectical dance. It became a daily after-dinner ritual with both of us determined to wear the other down with our stubbornness.

"But, Pa," I said, "you told me we should help those who are most needy."

"But you needn't choose the most dangerous place to help people. Look at the political situation in Nepal right now."

"But that's why they're in need, Pa!"

A few times we almost argued. Once, I think, we did. But he remained stoic mostly, an unimpressionable picture of wisdom. I adored his principled ways, his indifference to grand reasoning.

Then one night I said, "Remember Cambodia, Pa."

Just a few months earlier, I'd led a team of student leaders on a Youth Expedition Project through the Singapore International Foundation to paint classrooms and murals at an orphanage in Phnom Penh. On our first night, we stayed at a villager's home, a simple stilt house made of rattan and leaves. As I talked deep into the night with the host's daughter—Chantrea, who was exactly my age—it became clear that while she dreamt of being a doctor, unlike me she didn't have the means or opportunities to pursue that career. While I lived in a comfortable apartment, she lived on a farm struggling to survive.

As this realization dawned on us both, two strangers from worlds apart, we hugged each other tightly and cried our eyes red till we fell asleep. Then we bade goodbye the next morning, and our team moved to the orphanage.

The children there, tainted by frequent short visits by foreigners, were heartbreakingly patronizing, knowing exactly what to say or do to elicit special gifts from newcomers. "Hello, hello! You have sweets for me? Toy, maybe? Or camera?"

A boy named Kiry, far older in age than his height suggested, gave me a handmade gift. I looked at it, tearful. There in my hands lay a handmade kite, a symbol of freedom and dreams fashioned from a black plastic trash bag and sticks. It was all he owned, put into making a gift for me. Like Chantrea, he dreamt big dreams but had no means to reach them. The kite, a gift of disquieting contrasts, was a poignant reminder of that painful truth.

A month after I returned to Singapore, Chantrea wrote to me, *There is no rain. And my father is ill, so I have to work in the fields. I can never go to medical school.*

The injustice of her situation felt unacceptable, and my father and I decided to fundraise for her education. But the overseeing organization declined to accept our offer, citing problems they believed it would create for them—others might question why only Chantrea received the special privilege.

Visiting Cambodia forever ruined me for taking my easy life for granted. I kept my precious kite gift in my closet, taking it out from time to time. And now when I asked my father to remember Cambodia, his heart softened, and memories of his own growing up in a village, on a pineapple farm, and being hungry for days came rushing back. Even though he continued to say no, from the look in his eyes and the length of his pauses as the days went by, I could tell he was finally entertaining the possibility of allowing his daughter to visit a foreign country shaking with political instability.

Every night I prayed to God even though I didn't really know how. But again, Hebrews 11:1 had stood out to me: "Now faith is the substance of things hoped for, the evidence of things not seen." Was this faith? This blind believing in the impossible that God would send me to Nepal even though my circumstances pointed otherwise? It felt silly, kneeling on my bedroom floor talking to a God I'd never seen. Were all Christians this crazy?

A passage in the Bible gave me hope. In Matthew 17:20, when Jesus' disciples could not drive out demons from a demon-possessed boy and asked why, Jesus told them, "Because you have so *little* faith. Truly I tell you, if you have faith as *small* as a mustard seed, you can say to this mountain, 'Move from here to there,' and it will move. Nothing will be impossible for you" (NIV, emphasis added). I also discovered a similar passage, Luke 17:5–6. When Jesus tried to teach His disciples about forgiveness, they said, "Increase our faith!" Jesus replied, "If you had faith like a grain of mustard seed, you could say to this mulberry tree, 'Be uprooted and planted in the sea,' and it would obey you" (ESV).

Jesus rebuked the disciples for having "little faith," then promptly said that a mustard-seed–sized faith would be sufficient! The paradox left me in awe, and I learned that the disciples had a misplaced faith in themselves.[2] I received a revelation: God did not require me to summon more faith into my situation. Instead, He was inviting me to consider in *whom* my imperfect faith was placed.

I was relieved to realize that Jesus treasures a faith that is "real and trustful, though it be small and weak."[3] For no matter how we muster our own strength, it will never be sufficient for the God-sized dreams God places in our hearts. Only a humble faith placed rightly in God can harness the power of bringing those dreams to pass, even if they seem as impossible as the moving of mountains.

Later, as I matured as a Christian, I learned that Jesus chastised His disciples for having "little faith" on several occasions: when they doubted His provision (Matthew 6:25–34), when they were terrified by high winds and waves while in a boat during a storm (Matthew 8:23–26), when Peter took his eyes off Jesus and sank into the sea after also walking on water (Matthew 14:22–31), and when they failed to cast out a demon (Matthew 17:14–20). The Greek term *oligopistoi* renders colloquially to "tiny trusters" or "bitty believers."[4] They believed but couldn't fully trust Jesus to come through.

Do you often feel like that? A "tiny truster"? A "bitty believer"?

Perhaps Mark 9:24 aptly encapsulates our honest confession, "Lord, I believe; help my unbelief!" We believe, and yet we flounder in our faith. Even when we come blithely to God to increase our faith, God reminds us that a little faith placed in the right place—in Him—is all we really need. Our faith is not limited by our spiritual impotence. Rather, it is as powerful as the God in whom we place it.[5]

Back to the story. *God, if my going to Nepal is your will,* I prayed, *if you are the God who moves mountains, will you move my father's heart?*

As news of political unrest in Nepal continued to bubble, I convinced myself that God, not me, would have to persuade my parents to let me go.

One evening, my father's frown deepening into valleyed furrows, he said, "One of my staff told me a Christian Singaporean missionary serving in Nepal is returning to Singapore soon for a break. She wants to meet us and says she's willing to look out for you while you're there. . . ." His voice trailed off in the direction of his gaze as if he himself were shocked at how the impossible odds were falling in my favor.

My eyes widened. Was this his yes? Hope glimmered.

Two weeks later, my father and I met with the missionary over lunch. Moved by her story of radical dedication to rescuing women from the red-light districts of Nepal through her soap-making enterprise, his heart softened. Sending me to Nepal no longer seeming so farfetched to him, and he agreed to let me go.

Believe God for a Miracle Right Where You Are

As I grew older and recounted this story to people, I marveled at the incredulity of it all. What were the chances that my father, who owned just a tiny start-up company with merely five staff members, supervised one who knew of a missionary in Nepal, who in turn was soon returning to Singapore for a break, and wanted to meet with us and was willing to look out for me if I helped at that children's home?

That series of divine events culminated in my ultra-conservative—and again, pre-Christian—parents, who had never let me stay out later than ten at night (except once for prom!), saying yes. Truly, this was miraculous.

As a new Christian, I began to learn the meaning of faith, how by simply holding on to what God has deposited in our hearts, we can call forth into reality what may be unseen. Hebrews 11:3 says, "By faith we understand that the worlds were framed by the word of God, so that the things which are seen were not made of things which are visible."

When my father initially said no, I held on. And all I'd prayed was, *God, if my going to Nepal is your will, will you move my father's heart?*

Saying yes to God's promises amid the protests of those who most love you might not be easy, but it is simple. Faith makes room for what you pray for because you believe God will make it happen. It requires stoicism under pressure and crises, exhibiting calm. Faith is a persistent holding on to His promises. It's the quiet persistence of believing in what has not yet come to be. Yet despite its all-out, high-stakes commitment to believing, faith accepts whatever outcome God decides is best. *That's* what faith is!

Over the last decade, I've met many young people who had a desire—a dream—to help the poor overseas, but they knew their parents would flip if they did anything that risky. I've met women with a clear call of God on their lives who said their husbands would most certainly object. I've met men with dreams from God who said their wives would never agree to their pursuing them. People have said their children would retaliate or rebel.

It would be impossible to follow their dreams, they said.

My challenge to that perspective is this: if you believe your heavenly Father has called you to embark on a risk-filled venture, can't you also believe He can move the hearts of the people around you as you submit to His highest call? If you initially hear no from your earthly parents or loving spouses or children, will you conveniently accept it under the guise of honoring their wishes? Or will you hold on to that dream, pressing in through prayer, asking God to change hearts and let His will be done? And if your loved ones maintain their answer is no, will you trust God to provide enough grace and guide you into the fullness of His will nonetheless?

If there's one place to start believing God for a miracle, it's home—right where you are. So even when you hear no from family and loved ones, hold on. Persist in prayer. Believe in miracles. And dream brave.

FOR REFLECTION

1. What God-given dreams do you have trouble believing Him for?
2. What obstacles or protests stand in your way that make it challenging for you to hold on to your dreams?
3. How can you apply faith and prayer in your situation?

NEXT STEPS

1. Write down one or more dreams God has placed on your heart.
2. Make a list of several loved ones or friends who love to pray, then ask them to join your prayer team.
3. Schedule a fixed time every day to pray for people whose support you need to take bold steps forward in faith.

PRAYER

God, you know the dreams you've placed in my heart for your greater purposes. Yet I falter and fumble. When I imagine the reactions of those around me, fear and discouragement seep in. Will you speak to their hearts? Give me divine faith to hold on to the dreams you've given me. Give me courage to say yes to you, no matter what others say. Show me no dream is too small or too big when we surrender it to you. In Jesus' name I pray, amen.

2

say yes to God—again and again

> By faith we understand that the worlds were framed by the word of God, so that the things which are seen were not made of things which are visible.
>
> —Hebrews 11:3

MY DAUGHTERS, six and four as of this writing, have always loved make-believe. Even at around ages four and two, their world came alive when they spoke life into the mundane. "Mama," my firstborn would say while cradling an empty bowl, "this is yummy Chinese noodles—and *fishballs*!" My younger one would nibble on an invisible cookie in her chubby hands and declare, "*Dee*licious!" Even now, what is invisible comes to life through their spoken declarations. With an element of faith, what they can conjure becomes real to them.

Such is the power of faith in little children (Matthew 18:1–3). And such is the power of the spoken word. Except God's word is not make-believe. Hebrews 11:3 illustrates this profoundly, as it states that all that we know is fitted and framed by the "word of God." Not the personal word as in *logos* in Greek, but the spoken word *rhema*, the living, breathing, spoken word of God from which came the beginnings of the complex, glorious, magnificent world we know out of nothing.[1]

Similarly, our dreams come to life when we speak God's word into them and align them with His heart. It can be paralyzing to ponder the incredulity of a dream birthed from nothing, yet Hebrews 11:3 exhorts that, in our declarations, we release faith, which calls forth reality from the invisible, beckoning the formless to take shape.

Let me share this life-changing story that illustrates the power of speaking faith into impossible situations, resulting in extraordinary outcomes.

When God Calls, Will You Answer?

When I reached Nepal, any romanticism I'd harbored quickly dissolved as the thick smog in the air choked my lungs. Black soot coated everything, even my glasses. The city, a gray drab of concrete houses and messy roads, greeted me with loud honks. Imagine the relief I felt when I stumbled toward a three-story building with a little green garden and yellow mustard flowers, shielded from the animosity of the world by its tall concrete walls. Streams of children, all girls, tumbled out the door, shouting, "*Didi!* [big sister] *Didi!*" Their abounding joy amid stark poverty unraveled me.

I stood at the gate, eyes blinking. There I was—during a much-anticipated eight-month-long break after junior college (the equivalent of high school in America)—awaiting news of whether I'd been accepted to medical school, all while most of my friends were globe-trotting around Europe and America as one last holiday or interning at various companies before university started.

Had I made the right choice?

Before arriving, I'd learned that many of these girls had grown up with abuse. Yet two dozen little faces radiating like the sun looked at me, twinkling with curiosity, a welcome solace from the ashen world outside. I walked into the home gingerly, afraid to disrupt its usual rhythms. Outside, smoke billowed as rioters burned flags on the streets. But inside, the air pulsed with zeal as the children burst into Bible songs, exuberant and free.

On those winter nights, I shivered constantly. I rubbed my knees together trying to stay warm, but it was no use. Cold pierced into my aching bones. Hungry for warmth, I often snuck up to the kitchen around midnight to gobble down a bowl of cooked rice. But that didn't work either. *God*, I prayed, *I'm so cold. And so broken by these conditions. What am I doing here?*

I didn't know exactly why I was there, but my heart warmed with reassurance of God's good plans. I believed He knew what He was doing, and His peace stoked something deep within me I'd never known existed.

One ordinary morning, horrible news came—the home was being evicted from its rental. Countenances fell, and I stood in disbelief as chaos erupted around me. I soon learned eviction came every year. Once a local landlord discovered the children's home was connected to an overseas organization, they increased the monthly rent to an impossible sum.

I tried to help, but the children assured me they knew what to do. "It's okay, *Didi*. We've done this before." The girls, barely in their teens, dismantled their clunky bedframes and packed up heavy crockery all by themselves. Back home in Singapore, professional movers would be called in for a job like this. But here in Nepal, this massive endeavor was theirs alone.

I stood by a blue pickup truck at the front of the home, trying not to get in anyone's way. The older girls, with peculiar confidence, carried boxes stacked in their sinewy arms to heights above their heads like professionals.

The home had missionary parents of both genders, and Uncle Saba, one of the house fathers, walked to the truck in sweat-stained clothes. "We have to disenroll everyone at school," he told me, "and we have to find them a new school. Again!"

"But Aravi and Gauri have topped their standards," I said, meaning the two girls had each achieved first place in their cohorts. I had tears in my eyes as I stupidly stated the obvious.

"*Ke garne!* [What to do!]," he replied, tsk-tsking.

Three-year-old Shilpa tottered down the rocky dirt path with scrunched-up underwear in hand. She tossed her belongings onto the pickup with a flourish, then smiled gap-toothed at me. Her glazed-over eyes scanned the chaos again, and then, as if in utter resignation, she squatted by a wall and watched the familiar unfurling.

I nearly stopped breathing, and tears I'd fought so hard to keep back now rolled down my cheeks. Those in the world around me hustled and scurried, piled and stacked, while a shattering lay in my heart. How could this be happening?

As we all grieved our loss while trying to adjust to staying in a new, concrete structure that looked so mean with no grass or yellow flowers, I was tense with foreboding. The phone would ring, and I would think, *Who's evicting us now? Where are we moving to next?*

One night alone in my bed in the cold, dank basement, an awful weight on my chest rose and fell with every breath. I planted my face into my pillow, soaking it with tears. My heart throbbed with sorrow, then heaved with rage. I wanted to scream at this injustice, but only four gray walls stared back at me, four walls that also didn't belong to us.

Then I sensed God asking me, *Wai Jia, will you do more?*

Nothing in my bubble-wrapped life had prepared me for this. I feared what God might ask me to do, but I said, "Yes, Lord," aloud between sobs, my voice echoing. Then, as I closed my eyes, the drab basement disappeared. God opened my imagination to see endless sky with beautiful rainbow-colored kites soaring above the village plains below. *Start here*, I sensed God saying. *If you put your faith in Me, I'll show you what to do step by step.*

Each night after that, as I prayed with eyes closed to escape the drabness of the basement walls, a fresh painting emerged in my mind.

How Many Others Must Believe in Your Dream?

You might think you need a host of people to believe in your dream, but the next part of my story illustrates that's not necessarily true.

Six weeks later, the time came for me to leave Nepal for home. As Uncle Erick, the other house father and a Singaporean, drove me to the airport, silence lay between us like a fragile mirror. Then it broke, and we were left with only sharp pieces, memories of the traumatic move.

"The girls loved the craft activities you did for them, you know," he said.

"Really," I uttered back, distracted.

"Jes told me she wants to be a doctor like you do."

I finally came out of my stupor. "So how much would buying a permanent home for the girls cost?"

"Ha," he said with a sigh. "More than a hundred thousand dollars. Land prices here are insane. But we have no money, so this is what we have to deal with."

As I wheeled my luggage to the departure gate, my heart swelled, then nearly imploded. Like a crazy person, I spun around, ran back to Uncle Erick, and sputtered, "I have a dream!"

As soon as the words left my mouth, I was sure he would laugh—or worse, patronize me when I told him about my dream, cruelly encouraging me to pursue the idea though already convinced it would fail.

But he did not. "Tell me more," he said.

"I know this sounds stupid, even silly. And I know I'm just an eighteen-year-old girl with no credentials. But I feel God has given me this idea for a picture book—I could paint the illustrations—

and I just wonder if maybe we could sell it to raise enough funds to buy a permanent building. I know a hundred thousand dollars is a lot, and I'm really just nobody . . ."

I was babbling. And who was I kidding?

But with a steely glint in his eye, Uncle Erick looked into my soul and said in all seriousness, "I believe in your dream. I want you to meet with a man I know first thing when you get back to Singapore and share it with him." Then he handed me a piece of paper torn from his pocket notebook. He'd written the name of the man and his address on it, and I held it in my hands as though it was a golden Willy Wonka ticket.

I felt ridiculous. I didn't even have my university degree yet. I was just a little girl who liked to paint, even if poorly. But on the six-hour plane ride home, I sketched the entire story of a book I wanted to title *Kitesong*, and once home, I was eager to share my dream, this tremendous hope in my heart.

"Dad, I'm going to paint the illustrations for a book and raise funds with it for the girls in Nepal to have a home of their own."

Silence.

I searched his face for some affirmation, but he pressed his lips together tightly as if keeping words in while his mind searched for the right ones.

"This is a good idea," he finally said. "But . . ."

"But what?"

"The thing is, who would read or buy it? You have good intentions, Jia, but maybe the timing is not now. Maybe when you've built up your credentials, people will take note of you and what you've published."

My world caved in momentarily, but it was too late. Uncle Erick, the first person who listened to my dream, and then my college literature teacher, Mr. Ho, who encouraged me to take the next step, had already breathed faith into me and lit a little flame in my heart. Later in my life, my father, who first had doubts about my book *Kitesong*, became my greatest supporter in cheering me on to set up Kitesong Global as an international nonprofit.[2] I knew that even back then, his hesitation was a means of expressing his love.

So you see, it doesn't take many others to believe in your dream and offer encouragement to go on. Those who doubt you may even change their minds later on.

And although I didn't know much of the Bible as a new believer, Hebrews 11:3 had encouraged me that by faith, things that were once invisible would become seen. Even though *Kitesong* and a permanent home for the girls in Nepal had not yet come into being, by faith and the Word of God, I believed they would.

Let God Grow Your Faith Muscles

I started to paint, and on my nineteenth birthday the next day, I clutched Uncle Erick's paper and walked into a tall, foreboding catacomb of buildings. I found the man I was to approach, who turned out to be a senior pastor, and he referred me to his publisher.

Then I wandered through the quaint alleys of Chinatown amid haggling customers and gaudy wares until I found the address he'd given me—a nook in a shop house. I pushed the door open, hoping to be greeted by a receptionist.

No one. But stacks and stacks of books covered the wooden floors, and I could hear typing and the shuffle of human feet behind them.

"Hello? Is anyone here?" I called.

More typing and more shuffling.

"Hello, is anyone—"

A hunched-over figure, bristling with irritation, emerged from the landscape of books, his brow furrowed. "What do you want?" the man asked.

Stuttering, I explained why I was there.

"So you're the girl who went to Nepal while there were riots and bomb blasts there?"

He already knew about me, then. Did he know all about my book, *Kitesong* too?

"Yes. I am."

"Ah, okay. And you need help," he quipped.

Then, adjusting the round glasses perched precariously on his nose, he briefly leafed through my initial paintings. "These are pretty bad. If you can teach yourself to paint better, though, I'll sponsor two thousand copies of the book." I stood there speechless before this stranger, disbelief freezing me in place.

Then he said, "Okay, I'm quite busy now. See you next week."

"So I just come with more paintings?"

"Yeah. These aren't great, you know."

So far the book was nothing more than scrawls on paper. And the permanent home Uncle Erick and I had spoken of was but a figment of our imaginations, a desperate hope. I had nothing to hold on to except faith—the substance of things hoped for, the evidence of things unseen.

Still on my school break, night after night on my knees at home, I said the same prayer: *Dear God, will you make* Kitesong *happen and provide the girls with a permanent home?* Only by faith would this invisible dream be birthed into our present time, and I held on to my "title deed" of faith as a surety for the home.[3] I also sat in the aisles of the National Library, scouring dozens of watercolor books.

Day after day, I painted relentlessly from seven in the morning till ten at night. Then one day a week, I packed my new paintings into a plastic bag and made the long train ride to the publisher's office. Each time, my heart galloped. What would he say?

Then I'd tiptoe into his office, afraid to disturb the rhythmic hum of activity. "Hello? Is anyone here?"

But I need not have worried. Without a word, the publisher would appear from the city of stacked books and home straight into my paintings. He'd hold each one up to the light, shift his glasses, and scrutinize it, saying, "This one's okay," or, "This one's bad." Then finally he'd say, "Okay, this pile works, and this pile needs to be redone."

I'd look at him for some word of encouragement, some guidance to move forward, hungering for conversation. But as magically as he appeared, he disappeared. This publisher had rejected most of my paintings, tossing them into a heartbreaking pile. But I only painted more. I had no outlet for the anguish of witnessing the injustice of the girls' eviction other than those brushstrokes on paper.

Somehow, God had let me know our lives are the one chance we have to make a difference in this world. And we have the power to wield the strokes that determine the outcome of our dreams—if we're willing to say yes to Him again and again.

I often felt vexed—angry. All these years, I'd lived in ignorance at the world's complacency. I couldn't believe injustices like the one in Nepal had gone on, would continue to go on all over the globe forever. My emotions frightened me. I went to bed each night, mind racing, fearful of waking up to the puzzling disbelief that my world would keep spinning round and round unchanged while, in another world, thirty little lives struggled with the most basic of human rights—shelter—and with gaining an education. Did God care? I didn't want to wake up to the same tomorrows, soggy with yesterday's regrets with nothing changed.

I'd pray, *God, I have no idea what I'm doing. I don't even know the Bible. Why did I start on this foolish journey?* My faith wavering, I continued, *Are you there? How can I truly know you're real? If you are, will you prove it to me by breathing this impossible dream into being?*

My knuckles turned white from clenching my hands into fists, and tears streamed down my cheeks as I pleaded. *Not enough people believe in this dream, God. Is it your dream or merely mine? But if it's from you, make it happen. I'm willing to trust you even though I hardly know you. Please come through for me.*

I went to the business district one afternoon to meet a friend for lunch, and an incredulity consumed me there. I couldn't believe people were bent over staring at their phones, oblivious to the inequity I'd just witnessed in a world not so far away.

A dogged, punishing doubt swirled in my mind. What if all my efforts went to waste? It seemed like so many pieces of a gigantic puzzle would have to fall into place. Would *Kitesong* be published? Would people read it and sow into the cause? Would enough money be raised to purchase a home for the girls? Or by the time we had enough, would it be too late to avoid more anguish for them? Maybe the rental of the new building would be raised sooner than later and they'd be forced out once more. What if they had to disenroll from school again and then, feeling defeated, some of them dropped out completely, altering their futures forever?

Unending what-ifs rained down, but on one of the book's pages, I wrote, *There is a kitesong within me that will not be still.* The dream heaved and ebbed inside me, taking on a life of its own, as if God Himself put it there and my duty was to nurture it to fruition. So I continued to pray—crudely, passionately, as if all my life depended on it, believing if this dream didn't work out, life would be a farce and God a joker.

But no matter how hard I tried, how much I prayed, I heard nothing from God in return. Again, I often soaked my pillow with tears, once falling asleep on my knees.

I didn't realize it then, but God was growing my faith muscles little by little.

Keep Saying Yes

Perhaps like Mary, who was "troubled" when she first received God's promise through an angelic visitation and then yielded to His will (Luke 1:29–38), I willed myself to believe. Although I held no certainty of the outcome of my efforts, I was certain I had a duty to nurture, protect, and love the little dream growing inside my spiritual womb. While I could neither see nor hear God, the assurance that this dream was too magnificent for me to bear alone compelled me to believe it came from Him.

Three months after I first met the publisher, *Kitesong* was published. I hadn't known how this could happen, but God did.

The publisher shared the book with a circle of churches, and through word of mouth, a little spark grew into a roaring wildfire. I was shocked to be asked to speak at one of those churches.

"You want me to share? What do I say?"

"Just tell why you went to Nepal and painted *Kitesong*."

I had never sat on wooden pews before, much less addressed a crowd sitting on them. But I said yes.

As I told my story, my voice broke, and my hands trembled. I stood at the podium like a reed blowing in the wind, blood pulsing in my neck, certain those intelligent churchgoers would sniff me out and discover I hadn't grown up in church and had harbored so many doubts about God. I'm sure the color drained from my face as I saw dozens of blank faces staring at me.

Fortunately, God didn't care about my lack of confidence. Only later in my walk with Him did I learn how much He adores broken vessels, people who are little like me.

After my talk, I stood at the book table, shy and then speechless as people left checks for thousands of dollars for a stack of only ten or twenty books. And as the story spread through church bulletins, magazines, and then mainstream media, more than a hundred thousand dollars was raised within three months. I could hardly believe what God had done in spite of me. He was making, creating, and spinning His dream from what was once invisible into glorious reality (Hebrews 11:3).

The following year, I again visited the girls in Nepal.

"Sister Wai Jia, this is crazy," Uncle Saba said. In a little car and sometimes on a dusty scooter, he and I would scout out three-story cement houses perched on slopes, looking for the perfect home with a bit of green grass. A year later, the right home was purchased.

"This can only be the power of God," Uncle Erick said.

"*Didi,* thank you so much," said Tara, one of the oldest girls, blushing as she held a copy of *Kitesong.* "I want to study hard in this home and be a doctor like you."

Every two years or so, I visited again, looking forward to seeing the girls growing up. With time, they all blossomed with glory and beauty, glowing with the hope of a brighter future. The bold reality of a prayer-answering God changed them, and they, too, began to pray audacious prayers—asking to top their classes, pursue university learning, and engage in careers that would impact the world. They made me promise to bring my husband to visit whenever I got married, and ten years after my first visit, my husband, Cliff, came along.

In those ten years, many of the girls graduated to become preschool teachers. Some became bookkeepers. One became a nurse. Little Varsha, shaved bald in her early years because of persistent lice infestations in her hair, now shines with her beautiful tresses, exuding confidence. Even today I keep a photo collage of the girls in my living room. They're seated in nearly the same positions in a ten-year span, a reminder of what God could do through a simple, little dream He gave an eighteen-year-old.

All it took was a decision to say yes when the world said no. The miracle happened not by a fluke but because of a cumulative series of yeses—the initial yes to go to Nepal, then to paint, then to visit the publisher, and then to share about *Kitesong* with little public speaking experience. For the first time, I saw what God wants from us is not capability but availability. He wants our yeses, again and again, even when we don't believe in ourselves. A series of unabandoned yeses from a totally surrendered heart is what He looks for.

Through this experience, I saw that God is real, that He cares about the dreams He places in our hearts that cannot be stilled. However big or small we think those dreams might be, only He has the power to bring them to fruition according to His will.

Even when our dreams are but wispy hopes, our sure confidence in God matters, and it was for this kind of incredible faith that the ancients were commended: "By [their faith] the elders obtained a good testimony" (Hebrews 11:2).

If we believe our God spoke the universe into existence from nothingness (Genesis 1:3), can't we believe He will make the invisible, visible? As you dream brave, will you say yes to Him—however many times it takes?

FOR REFLECTION

1. What makes believing in your dreams challenging?
2. How can you apply God's truths to the discouragements you face?
3. In which areas of your life do you need a greater measure of trust and obedience to help you say continual yeses to God?

NEXT STEPS

1. Write about an incident when God's faithfulness came through for you and the invisible was made visible.
2. List Bible verses that describe the faithfulness of God. For example, "He who calls you is faithful, who also will do it" (1 Thessalonians 5:24).
3 Write down what you will say yes to so God can help you begin your journey of faith concerning your dream. Then share that with a trusted friend or mentor.

PRAYER

God, trusting in you can be hard. Believing in a dream that has yet to come to fruition can be tough. Yet by faith I declare our world was formed at your command and the invisible was made visible. Give me strength to say yes to you as often as you ask. Grant me a willing spirit to be open to your guidance. Increase my surrender and trust in you to bring the seemingly impossible to pass, to make the invisible visible. As I say continual yeses to you, I declare your will to be done. In Jesus' name I pray, amen.

3

believe that your pain has purpose

> By faith Joseph, when he was dying, made mention of the departure of the children of Israel, and gave instructions concerning his bones.
>
> —Hebrews 11:22

YOU SHOULD DIE. *You're worthless.*

When the voices began taunting me, I ran—literally. Jogging helped me escape. But what started as a harmless coping tool quickly morphed into a savage slave master. Exercise became an addiction, and then avoiding food became an opiate. I imprisoned myself in a cage—my own body. And as my hair fell out in sheets and my monthly periods stopped, fear tightened its grip on me.

"Your scan shows you have the bone density of a sixty-five-year-old." The nurse's puzzled tone frightened me. Why did I, now a twenty-year-old, have a hip fracture with no prior accident? But I knew full well why. Because of my severe weight loss, my body was breaking down.

The voices persisted: *You're worthless.*

In the dark nights, all alone in my university dormitory, I peered over the edge of the balcony outside my room, then closed my eyes. *You are a pathetic Christian,* said the voices. After powerfully experiencing God through painting and publishing *Kitesong* and then hearing His call to be a medical missionary during a follow-up visit to the children's home in Nepal, I couldn't understand how I'd fallen so far.

As I contemplated the long jump down, a vision emerged in the darkness. I stood on a stage sharing my recovery story with a large audience in America. *What?* I scoffed at my own presumptuousness. After all, I was just a nobody, a little Asian girl from a tiny red dot on the world map called Singapore. I had a Chinese name people struggled to remember. *You're nobody,* came the voices again, confirming my assessment.

But the vision kept me alive, lighting a renewed faith in my heart, and God spoke to me: *Your life is worth the world to Me.*

While I was so ill, I drew inspiration from Joseph, a man with a life that makes for riveting, Hollywood-quality movie drama. In the book of Genesis, beginning in chapter 36, we're told that at the age of seventeen he had two miraculous dreams where sheaves and the sun, moon, and stars all bowed to him, symbolizing his parents and eleven brothers doing so. This was an amazing picture of his future! In fact, it was a promise.

But shortly after, his jealous brothers sold him to the Egyptians as a slave, and then in a twist of events, he was bought by Potiphar, Pharaoh's officer. Joseph served him faithfully, but through no fault of his own, he was maligned, thrown into prison, and forgotten.

Yet because of the divine favor he had in dream interpretation, he was summoned out of prison to interpret Pharaoh's dreams. Joseph's predictions came true, and only twenty-two years after his brothers sold him as a slave, they and Joseph's parents bowed down to him at last, just like in his initial dreams.

You might relate to this story if you, like me, hold on to dreams that have yet come to pass.

In Hebrews 11:22, we're told Joseph gave specific instructions about his burial in the promised land, because even on his deathbed he believed that God would take Israel there (Genesis 50:24–25).[1] He believed even when he couldn't see the outcome. In the same way, we must hold on to God's promises and take action toward them in faith even when we can't see the end.

In our journey of pursuing our God-given dreams, setbacks are certain. In fact, after God plants a dream in our hearts, spiritual warfare begins (1 Peter 5:8). We might be bewildered by the chaos and even depression that besiege us, but Joseph's life shows us this is not an unexpected trajectory. Unfettered by life's trauma and injustices, this man remained full of faith. He never gave up.

You might relate to the ups and downs of Joseph's life just as I did. At times, you might even feel like giving up. But I encourage you to hold on to God's promises through your pain and use it to develop the kind of faith that trusts God for promises—even those that may come *beyond your lifetime*. Joseph believed God would restore Israel to the promised land even though it wouldn't happen until four hundred years later (Joshua 24:32).[2] Despite all his setbacks—being kidnapped, enslaved, accused, and jailed—Joseph allowed God to use them as launchpads for His eternal inheritance, serving God and saving his own family line and that of Jesus.

As we embrace our setbacks, can we trust that God lets nothing go to waste? For He uses our pain to mold us for His eternal inheritance. Like Joseph, we must press on toward our ultimate goal of inheriting God's good promises for us with future generations.

Let me tell you more of the story about my illness, hoping to encourage you to embrace your own setbacks as launchpads in claiming your eternal inheritance.

Trust God Even When Your Life Falls Apart

Right after the miracle of *Kitesong*, a crisis hit my father's business. We sold my childhood home and downsized. And my older sister moved overseas. My life was falling away parts at a time. What was happening?

Trying to cope amid my anxiety, and now in university studying medicine, I exercised relentlessly. I paced up and down my dormitory room. Enjoying food became like treason. In the night, the pain from my bones jutting out from my hips kept me awake. My grades suffered. And as I shared earlier, voices in my head told me I was worthless and should die. Self-hatred consumed me.

Trapped in a battle against the fulfillment of God's promises, I began to doubt Him again. I asked myself if God was real, and if He'd really called me to love the poor as a medical missionary. If so, I wondered, why was I going through this? Little did I know how depression and anorexia, the very things that should sink me, would become two of the experiences God would use most powerfully in my life.

One day a mentor challenged me. "Why don't you get help?"

I merely pursed my lips, stubborn.

"If the doctor assesses that you're well, you won't need further therapy. Why not just go for a first appointment?"

Giving in, I did and was told, "You have severe depression and a serious eating disorder. You need to be admitted to this hospital."

"Please don't," I pleaded. "My classmates are doing clinical rotations here, and I don't want them to find out."

Thankfully, the doctor relented. But over the course of an intensive year of outpatient therapy, I wondered how I could be a doctor if I was a patient.

Shame wrapped its dark cloak around me, and I thought, *It would be easier to die.*

Then I heard God ask, *Why don't you paint?*

Deep down, I knew He wanted me to publish more of my paintings as a picture book and speak up against the stigma of mental health. The same vision of me speaking hope to an international audience flashed in my mind, strengthening my resolve to live. So I painted and developed that new book. But when the time came for *A Taste of Rainbow* to be published, people cautioned me.

"Don't do it. What will everyone think of you?"

"Your past will haunt you in public forever."

"How will this affect your credibility as a doctor?"

While riding a bus one afternoon, I panicked, overwhelmed. I called my publisher, the donor sponsoring the printing of the books, and even my psychologist. But none of them gave me a clear answer.

"Just decide," said one of them with irritation.

"How can I?"

"You're over twenty-one years of age."

"I don't know what to do."

"Just decide. Gotta go."

Click.

Sitting on that bus with a tearstained cell phone in my hand, I felt like an orphaned five-year-old, desperately wanting a parent to help me process the avalanche of fears and anxieties amid adult considerations in a frightening world. I looked at the sky through the windows and felt the world bearing down on me, almost crushing me.

I was on my own.

But then I considered how Joseph felt when thrown into a pit and sold into slavery, then being falsely maligned by Potiphar's wife and imprisoned. He was all alone too. As the bus chugged on, a vision of me again speaking on a stage flashed in my mind.

God's embrace enveloped me, and I felt Him say, *Trust Me*. I'd imagined Joseph's loneliness, but now I imagined his hope, fanned into flame, when he remembered his dreams of the sheaves, sun, moon, and stars bowing to him.

The vision God gave me infused me with courage. Even if others didn't truly support me, I knew He would.

Compelled by the vision of the Israelites returning to the promised land, Joseph acted in faith to specify his burial in Canaan as a symbol of his joined interest in their inheritance. Likewise, against all my fears, God gave me the courage to step out. A holy desperation to see the impact of my courage transform future generations arrested me. Like Joseph, I decided I would hold on to the vision and take a concrete step of faith forward. I would publish *A Taste of Rainbow* as a symbol of my faith in God's healing power throughout the generations.

And with God's help, I did.

On my twenty-fourth birthday, and now in medical school, I received a phone call from the press. "We'd like to interview you about your new book."

My heart beating fast, I glowed with pride. I thought, *How good God is to fulfill my dream of using my pain to help others, especially on my birthday!* My psychiatrist and psychologist both agreed to attend the interview as a show of support and to ensure that I, as an ongoing patient, was protected.

But events took a different twist that day. Any rapport I tried to build with the reporter interviewing me hit the ground hard like bricks. "How much weight did you lose?" I was asked. "What did you do? How bad was it?" Each question grew in force and fury, gathering menace as it traveled across the table to me when I couldn't answer. The hospital had said I couldn't share such details as it could be triggering to readers who might be struggling.

My mouth dried up, and slowly, my smile drained away. My eyes searched the faces of my psychologist and psychiatrist. Why weren't they protecting me like they said they would? I felt cut by betrayal.

Then a grave realization dawned on me. This was not an interview to celebrate my resilience but a ploy to send a sensational story of a doctor-to-be-turned-patient viral.

The interview ended like a comma in mid-sentence. Later, well into the evening, my phone kept buzzing with calls from that same reporter.

"Tell me how much you weighed before and after. My editor wants the details."

"I can't. I'm not allowed to."

The probing questions morphed into a menacing threat when at a quarter to midnight, the reporter said, "If you don't give me what I ask for, we'll drop your story. And everything you did—*everything*—will be a waste."

Everything will be a waste.

Alone in my dormitory room, exhausted from a disastrous twenty-fourth birthday, I sank to my knees in tears. I emailed my pen pal at the time—my future husband, Cliff—and wrote *A terrible way to turn twenty-four*. The very day God made to celebrate my birth and His promises for my life had come under siege. This was no coincidence but an intentional ambush.

Cliff immediately phoned. "Genesis 50:20 says, 'You meant evil against me; but God meant it for good, in order to bring it about as it is this day, to save many people alive.'" These were the words of Joseph, the character from the Bible God had been using to inspire perseverance through my pain.

"*A Taste of Rainbow* will not be a waste, Wai Jia," Cliff said.

As the weeks went by, the book received some local publicity. I spoke at conferences, but without wider publicity, they paled in trifling comparison to the vision I'd seen. For years, that reporter's words echoed in my head: *Everything will be a waste.*

God Fulfills His Promises

Seven years later, at the age of thirty-one, as I pursued a Master of Public Health at Johns Hopkins University in the States, I remembered the vision of me speaking on a stage about *A Taste of Rainbow* and found my way to a renowned eating disorder specialist. I was excited to share the book with her.

"This is *nice*," she said vacuously. "But I have many such patient projects. This is not special."

This is not special. Everything will be a waste.

The voices echoed in my head, and I wanted to disappear. I went home, wept, and asked God, *Did you forget your promise?* I felt tormented by the ups and downs of life.

Weeks later, one afternoon my cell phone rang. A woman from Nashville, Tennessee, a former marketing director for one of the best Christian record labels in America, chirped, "Will you come speak at our Hungry for Hope conference?"

Stunned, I held back. The chances of my being available to speak at her event were slim. And I was sure that as soon as she heard more of my foreign accent, she'd have second thoughts anyway.

"How did you get my contact information?"

"A friend of mine is a clinical psychologist. She's a relative of a faculty member at Johns Hopkins who picked up a copy of *A Taste of Rainbow* from your supervisor's desk. I searched for the book online and felt this stirring in my heart telling me you need to share your story in America."

My jaw could have hit the floor.

"What would you like me to speak about?"

"What do you feel led to speak about?"

"My life message is about how God sets our dreams free."

She exploded, "Dreams! Can you believe it? Dreams!"

I envisioned her leaping across the room giving high fives to an invisible crowd around her. "That's the theme of our conference!"

she squealed. "We've been praying for a keynote speaker for months. It's *you*! You and your family are coming to Nashville!"

As God would have planned it, the conference date was a month after my graduation from Johns Hopkins.

As I stood before thousands of people in Nashville, speaking about how God takes the littlest of our dreams and breathes life into them, I marveled at His ways. Genesis 50:20 came to mind, when Joseph said to his brothers, "You meant evil against me; but God meant it for good, in order to bring it about as it is this day, to save many people alive."

Because of that strategic conference, God opened doors for *A Taste of Rainbow* to be used in treatment centers around the world. Opportunities for me to speak internationally opened up. The book was reprinted twice. Youth around the world wrote to me sharing how the book inspired them to recover from their own mental struggles. The enemy meant to use the eating disorder and depression to destroy my life, but God meant them for good. In John Piper's words about Joseph's brothers, "They do not know that in the very effort to destroy this dreamer, they are fulfilling Joseph's dreams."[3]

Hebrews 11:22 thus reminds us of the steadfast faith we must keep to the very end. How high are the stakes for our unbelief! Without the faith to dream brave, we may miss the joining of an eternal inheritance with generations beyond our earthly deaths, forfeiting legacies beyond our lifetimes.

Are you suffering through illness, injustice, or trauma? Know this: your pain has a purpose. Psalm 119:71 says, "It is good for me that I have been afflicted, that I may learn Your statutes." While we can let pain drive us away from God, we can also let it propel us toward Him. When we persevere in our pain and enter into the fellowship of Christ's sufferings (Philippians 3:10), we become part of God's battalion against the enemy, choosing to claim victory as a testimony to a broken world no matter the circumstances. Our setbacks can be the very launchpads upon which God propels us into our destinies.

Joseph's life is a testament to this truth. God didn't compensate him by salvaging the bad in his life. Instead, God used precisely that bad to mold and train him for the ultimate destiny of favor. You may have received dreams, visions, promises, and prophecies from God a long time ago and are wondering how far you've strayed away from fulfilling them. Yet Joseph waited twenty-two years for God's dreams to be fulfilled in his life, and his faith to believe in God for an event that would happen four hundred years after his death shows God's plans cannot be thwarted. What man means for evil in your life can be God's design for a greater good.

Will you trust God will use your pain in His grand destiny for you? Will you dream brave because of that?

FOR REFLECTION

1. With what setbacks have you struggled?
2. How have these setbacks made you stronger?
3. What's at stake if you don't act in faith? Think about the generational implications as well.

NEXT STEPS

1. In the first column of a chart like this one, list lies you've believed about yourself. You may take inspiration from the examples given.

Lies I've believed about myself:	**What God says about me:**	**Verses that prove God's Word:**
I am a coward.	I am bold.	God has not given us a spirit of fear, but of power and of love and of a sound mind (2 Timothy 1:7).

2. Spend some time with God in worship, perhaps listening to some quiet music. What do you sense Him saying about you? Write that down in the second column and then declare it aloud.
3. In the third column, list Bible verses you can use to counteract the lies you've been believing.

PRAYER

God, you know my struggles, and I'm weary walking with these shackles. Will you free me from these chains and renew my mind? Help me hold on to the visions, dreams, promises, and prophecies you have for me and to persevere through trial. Give me faith like Joseph had to take action even when I can't see the outcome. Turn my pain into purpose and my bondage into freedom for future generations. In Jesus' name I pray, amen.

4

hide in the refuge of prayer

> By faith Moses, when he was born, was hidden three months by his parents, because they saw he was a beautiful child; and they were not afraid of the king's command.
>
> —Hebrews 11:23

"THAT'S ENOUGH!" I snapped.

As my three-year-old wailed inconsolably, refusing to be strapped into her car seat, my five-year-old began to whine, "Mama! Mama!" Hungry and tired, I lost my cool.

"Your sister is refusing to be reasoned with, but I trust *you* understand. Now, not a word more."

My firstborn raised her voice to be heard over her bawling sister. "But Mama, I—"

"*Enough!*" I announced.

Silence.

Cliff started driving off, and pleased with myself, I had just turned back to glare at my firstborn when she whimpered, her eyes wide with panic. "You forgot to strap *me* in, Mama."

I jumped in my seat, and Cliff jolted the car to a halt. Then I cupped my mouth, filled with repentance.

"I am so sorry, sweetheart. Was that what you were trying to tell me all this while?"

"Yes."

As I got out of the car to buckle Sarah-Faith in, my face flushed. Cliff and I had taught our children the principles of obedience on a daily basis. "Obey, and obey at once," they would recite back to us. "Or else, you'll get a spanky!" one of them would tease at times.

But this time Sarah-Faith knew better. Instead of obeying my command to stay silent, she put her fears aside to obey a higher command she inherently knew was right—the traffic and safety rules. I looked into her eyes, pooled with assurance, and smiled at her faith to do what was right, her courage to yield to a higher authority even at the risk of being reprimanded. Even though it was against what she had learned, she knew it was for a higher purpose that was worth it.

On the drive home, the Lord brought to my mind the few times Cliff and I had to make key decisions that overturned common logic and went "against authority" to stay true to God's will for our lives. It felt counterintuitive—sinful even—since the Bible is replete with commands to obey our authorities. Hebrews 13:17 states, "Obey those who rule over you, and be submissive, for they watch out for your souls, as those who must give account." Romans 13:1 tells us, "Let every soul be subject to the governing authorities. For there is no authority except from God, and the authorities that exist are appointed by God." And Titus 3:1 and 1 Peter 2:13–15 remind us to be "subject to rulers and authorities" for "the Lord's sake."

Obeying authority is clearly a biblical instruction. Yet God calls us higher. When the laws of man clash with the laws of God, He expects us to heed His higher authority at the risk of even our very lives. Hebrews 11:23 makes this real: "By faith Moses, when he was born, was hidden three months by his parents, because they saw he was a beautiful child; and they were not afraid of the king's command."

In Moses' day, the children of Abraham, Isaac, and Jacob were quickly forming a prosperous nation of twelve tribes, attracting fear, jealousy, and spite from the Egyptians (Exodus 1:7–9). As such, the king—or pharaoh—enslaved the Hebrews, afflicting them with hard bondage (vv. 11–14). But they did not relent.

When those methods failed, the king commanded the midwives to kill all newborn baby boys. But Exodus 1:17 tells us that instead of obeying the authorities of the time, the "midwives feared God, and did not do as the king of Egypt commanded them, but saved the male children alive." Because of their fear of God, God rewarded them, provided households for them, and "the people multiplied and grew very mighty" (verse 20). How interesting that for a blatant disregard for authority, God blessed the midwives. And because of that, the Israelites prospered.

Out of desperation, Pharaoh commanded the ultimate genocide —for all the people, not just the midwives, to cast every son born into the river (verse 22). And in this atmosphere of deep-seated hatred and hostility, Moses' parents decided not to heed authority. In an intentional act of courage and faith, they hid Moses. Hebrews 11:23 even tells us explicitly that "they were not afraid of the king's command" even though disobeying him was likely to cost them their lives.

While I certainly want my children to obey us, I also want them to discern rightly. When I forgot to strap Sarah-Faith into her car seat, her resistance to my command to stay silent protected her life. In the same way, as we pursue our God-given destinies to fulfill His dreams for our lives, I believe God wants us to seek Him so intimately that we will be able to confidently discern His voice even if it calls for the unusual overturning of human authority placed above us. His voice must, after all, supersede that of man's (Acts 5:29). In Moses' case, the stakes for failing to do so were high. It involved an entire generation and beyond.

Moses' parents hid their son to protect and guard his life. When they saw he was "exceeding fair" (Acts 7:20 KJV)—or "beautiful in God's sight" (ESV)—they "doubtless through a divine presage of things to come, and not merely from his beauty, believed that God had designed him for some singular usefulness."[1] So they hid Moses till they could no longer, then released him into the river in a basket.

When we're under siege by authorities in our lives, are we willing to hide our dreams under the protection of prayer until we sense God's release—even if it means taking a risk to obey His higher authority?

Hide Your Dreams under Prayer

I once had to "hide" a dream under prayer when my parents objected to it. In many parts of Asia, children live with their parents until they marry, as a way of expressing filial piety. Obeying parental authority is a deep part of honoring the culture, hierarchy, and social milieu of Asian community. Overturning that authority can have far-reaching and complicated implications.

"No," my father said. "Cliff doesn't even have enough savings for himself. What kind of future can you see with him?"

My parents asked, "Don't you have any suitors from medical school?"

They went on. "Besides, he's had a liver transplant. That's so . . . high-risk. Didn't you just say he had a liver crisis recently?"

I shut the door to my bedroom behind me. Then as I huddled in a corner, my tears ran like a waterfall. I texted my mentors. Some of them had also expressed concerns about my relationship with Cliff when his liver enzyme markers skyrocketed. This event had alarmed his specialists enough for them to order a biopsy to investigate the possibility of cancer recurrence.

"I've had the liver transplant for over twenty years," Cliff told me. "Maybe it's given up on me."

That was the last thing I wanted to hear from the man who had proposed to me, the man I believed God had chosen to be my husband.

Our love story was an impossible fairy tale turned true. Who would have thought that a Google search with the words *Christian triathlete* so I could learn more about my newfound sport interest would lead me to Cliff's blog? *I had cancer when I was ten*, he'd shared. *God saved me through a liver transplant. I completed an Ironman, and I desire to pursue missions.*

Tears pricked the corners of my eyes as I read the inspirational story of a cancer survivor who loved the Lord and sold everything he had to be a missionary in the field. Blown away by Cliff's testimony, I left a comment: *Your life is such an inspiration. Keep living for Jesus!*

Little did I know that ten thousand miles away in frosty Canada, worlds away from tropical Singapore, Cliff would trace that comment to my blog.

I'm so encouraged by your life's dream to serve the poor too, he wrote.

Your wife looked so happy when you won that medal, I wrote back, referring to his profile picture.

That photo? That's not my wife. I'm not even attached! That was a fellow medalist who was so ecstatic that she kissed me on the podium!

Who was this guy? What if he stalked people online? What if he controlled cyber-syndicates or organized fraudulent online transfers and love scams? Yet something about the naivete and transparency in his writing kept me writing back. But after nearly two months of email correspondence with this man whose family had immigrated to Canada from Hong Kong when he was a child, the burden of a developing friendship weighed on me. What was I doing?

I called my mentor at church. "I have something to share with you in person."

"Over lunch?" she asked. "How's Japanese?"

I took a deep breath. It was time to come clean. Clearly, I'd crossed a line. I shouldn't even have responded to Cliff in the first place.

As we waited for sushi, I passed my mentor a printout of our email exchanges. Then as she fingered the sheets, I examined the crease between her eyebrows and awaited her verdict. Why wasn't I strong enough to stop writing on my own? Why did I choose to wait for my mentor to tell me the obvious? I should have had the sense to put an end to this friendship that would surely be unfruitful.

"Wow." She looked up. "You should keep writing. This is an unusual way of meeting someone, but I have a good feeling about it."

"What? Are you crazy?"

"I'll pray about it, and you should too. But I feel the Holy Spirit is guiding this."

Cliff and I continued what still seemed like a bizarre friendship as pen pals. Once he wrote, "Would you be my ministry partner?"

Thick with naivete, I asked a good friend of mine, "What do you think he means?"

"He's proposing to you, duh!" she said.

I felt my face blushing, unwilling to admit how this unlikely friendship was blossoming into something more.

Then months later, Cliff and his church friends signed up for a mission trip to Cambodia. *Could I swing by Singapore to visit?* he asked.

My stomach lurched. Stunned, I deferred to my mentors. If they said no, declining would rest easy on my conscience. But to my shock they said yes. "It's time, Wai Jia."

Cliff showed up over my birthday weekend, and during his three-day visit, I fiercely guarded my heart. After all, he would soon depart, and I didn't want to promote any expectations.

But against my own wishes, I was slowly falling for this man, and my heart felt torn to pieces. I loved Cliff's gentleness, love for God, and megawatt smile. But how could we be together—marry?

We lived on opposite poles of the earth. Each of our lives had its own trajectory. Then my heart grew with resentment. *God, why did you let this happen?*

The next morning, Cliff texted, *Goodbye. I loved our time together.*

Mixed feelings swirled in my gut. A part of me grieved at his leaving while another desperately wished we'd never met. I threw my anxiety into prayer. *Lord, will you give me a sign if Cliff is meant to be someone special in my life?*

Two hours later, my phone buzzed with a text from a familiar number. *I'm still here! The plane broke down. Free to meet?*

I stared at the phone, incredulous. Was he joking?

Yet I hardened my heart. Developing our friendship further would only lead to heartbreak. Determined not to lead him on, I arranged a dinner for him with a male missionary friend.

But then my friend phoned. "I'm so sorry, Wai Jia! My student broke his foot, and I'm on the way to the hospital. Cliff isn't replying to my messages—he may have left his phone at his hotel—so you'll have to meet him at the café instead!"

I dragged my feet grudgingly, my mind racing. How could this have happened?

Unwittingly, I fell into our first date. We chatted late into the night, discovering we had more in common than we thought.

Goodbye again, Cliff texted the next morning before his flight.

I prayed, *God, will you give me a second sign to confirm Cliff's place in my life?*

Two hours later, my phone buzzed again. My eyes widened in disbelief as I read, *The plane is full of passengers from the previous day's breakdown. There were three seats available and four of us. So they kicked me out! Free to meet again?*

As Cliff walked me home after dinner that evening, I caught a glimpse of a familiar hunched-over shadow in a dirty corner of the train station. It was Grandpa Chee, an elderly, crippled busker who played the harmonica. A year earlier, I'd led him to Christ.

"Wanna say hi?" I asked Cliff as I nodded toward my friend.

I'd brought other friends to meet Grandpa Chee, and the air would freeze and conversations would be stilted. A previous suitor even cringed when he caught a whiff of Grandpa Chee's old clothes. But not with Cliff. With the ease of someone used to conversing with the poor, Cliff knelt beside him and even spoke his dialect.

My heart swelled. I'd asked for another sign, and there before my eyes God showed me Cliff's authenticity, his heart for the poor. Tears rolled off my cheeks as the two men chatted late into the night.

That evening, as I witnessed Cliff's sincerity in serving the poor, he won my heart. To this day, we joke that God had to interfere with two flights just to make His point clear to me!

Cliff and I both continued to pray. Would he move to Singapore? Would God call us to serve in two different countries? Neither of us knew what was next.

Obey a Higher Order

One day I received this email from Cliff: *I applied to a mission organization with sixty-five offices around the world. They don't know a thing about you. Of all places, they've posted me to their headquarters in Singapore!*

Through this series of divine coincidences and overcoming impossible odds, God made our way together clear. But then came the biggest objection from my parents: "If you marry Cliff, aren't you afraid of being widowed early because of his transplant and its potential problems?" Their daily interrogations rained on me like nails.

Proverbs 6:20 says, "Keep your father's command, and do not forsake the law of your mother." To obey my parents, to bow to their wishes, would end my relationship with Cliff at once. Yet a higher order beckoned us to lay our relationship before God and not sever it. And so holding hands in prayer till they were white-knuckled, we surrendered our relationship to Him. Led by the Holy Spirit, Cliff and I also embarked on a Daniel Fast.

We'll pray for you, texted our mentors in both Canada and Singapore.

"Fast and pray together," a mentor couple encouraged us. As an interracial couple, they, too, had initially encountered vehement objections to marrying.

Instead of confronting my parents with arguments and accusations, we, like Moses' parents hid him, hid our relationship under prayer, protecting our resolve to obey His call for us to pursue a missional life together.

"Lord, will you let your will be done?" we prayed.

Day after day, my parents pressed me for an answer, making it clear what they wanted. I begged God for grace. Then on the twenty-second day of our Daniel Fast, something changed. They asked, "Does Cliff need help finding a place to stay in Singapore long-term?"

I could not believe my ears. They were now open to my continuing relationship with Cliff, knowing it would no doubt lead to marriage.

I called Cliff at once and said, "God answers prayer!"

The truth is, saying yes to God may not be straightforward. While He desires us to obey authority, there may be times, though few and far between, when He calls us to abandon authority to yield to His higher calling.

How can we discern this rightly? In his book *Experiencing God*, Henry Blackaby tells us that "the Holy Spirit will use the Bible, prayer, circumstances and other believers to speak to you."[2] In other words, wisdom gained through God's Word, revelation through prayer, uncanny circumstances revealing His divine hand, and a multitude of counselors from our church community (Proverbs 15:22) can guide us.

Ask yourself if you're resisting authority with a heart of rebellion or with a heart of yieldedness to your King. As you develop an intimate prayer life with God, may His peace be your sure guide. And when you hear His voice, may you have the courage to obey it.

Just as Jesus left His parents' side without permission to be in His Father's house, there may be times He calls you to Himself (Luke 2:49). No one knows if God spoke to Jesus' or to Moses' parents in an audible voice. The Bible doesn't say. Perhaps all they had was an intimate relationship with Him to follow what He impressed on their hearts.

We, too, must develop that intimacy with God. What Moses' parents did changed the course of history forever, saving their son to lead the Israelites out of bondage.

As you wisely hide certain dreams under the refuge of prayer, may God give you His wisdom to listen keenly, discern rightly, act bravely—and if necessary, to obey His higher order. Following His lead, you, too, could change history.

FOR REFLECTION

1. What kind of tensions have you struggled with between yielding to human authority and God's authority?
2. Write down your fears and concerns about resisting human authority to follow God in your life.
3. What were some principles you applied to help you discern rightly?

NEXT STEPS

1. Write down the names of any mentors you can trust to pray for you, give you honest advice, and keep you accountable.

2. List two of the worst possible consequences of forgoing human approval to seek God's approval.
3. Spend a few minutes in prayer asking God to give you a heart of yieldingness and intimacy with Him.

PRAYER

God, I commit my life into your hands. Will you help me guard and protect the dreams you've given me under the refuge of prayer? Will you give me the courage to yield to your plans even when I come under siege by human authority? Grant me wisdom to discern rightly, that I may not resist authority because of my rebellion but out of divine obedience to you. In Jesus' name I pray, amen.

5

give God your all

> Without faith it is impossible to please Him, for he who comes to God must believe that He is, and that He is a rewarder of those who diligently seek Him.
>
> —Hebrews 11:6

ONE NIGHT, as Cliff and I pondered how our wedding could be a blessing to others, we both sensed God speaking to us: *Will you give away all your wedding proceeds to the poor?*

We looked at each other, incredulous, and I fought back tears. I'd always dreamt of having a perfect garden wedding, and nursed over years of adolescent wonder, that vision had taken on an unreal quality. At Asian weddings, couples typically recoup the cost of hosting an extravagant wedding and gain added financial security at the onset of marriage through *ang bao*s—red packets with love gifts of money. Culturally, this is auspicious, a good omen for starting a life of bliss and abundance. And with Cliff having sold all he had and poured his savings into serving as a missionary, plus the high cost of garden venues, God knew we needed the money.

But if we did as He asked, my dream wedding wouldn't be possible. And we wouldn't have the financial security an overflow of gifts would provide.

Matthew 6:19–20 came to my mind: "Do not lay up for yourselves treasures on earth, where moth and rust destroy and where thieves break in and steal; but lay up for yourselves treasures in heaven." As I shared this with Cliff, he pointed out verse 33: "Seek first the kingdom of God and His righteousness, and all these things shall be added to you."

God was asking me if I was willing to seek first His kingdom's purposes. If I trusted Him. If I would take this step of faith. As Cliff and I continued to scour the Word about faith, Hebrews 11:6 stood out: "Without faith it is impossible to please Him, for he who comes to God must believe that He is, and that He is a rewarder of those who diligently seek Him." And in the verses before and after Hebrews 11:6, the Word describes examples of people from the Old Testament who displayed faith in God even when they couldn't see the outcome. Abel, Enoch, Noah, Abraham, Sarah—they all obeyed God even though the fulfillment of His promises seemed distant.

Like our fathers of faith, we could not see the outcome. *What reward could there possibly be, Lord?* I asked as I shrugged, disappointed. Yet God continued to say, *Will you put your faith in Me? Will you trust My reward by diligently seeking Me?*

Matthew 7:11 states, "If you then, being evil, know how to give good gifts to your children, how much more will your Father who is in heaven give good things to those who ask Him!" Hebrews 11:6 thus reminds us of God's faithfulness—when we seek Him, He *will* reward us. He does that simply because of who He is. So when God beckons us to put our faith in Him, can we believe that He has good things in store for us, as a heavenly Father would, even when we can't see the outcome? To those with faith, the future reward God has for us is present![1]

I felt God speak to my spirit, *I want an all-out, radical, abandoned surrender that does not turn back. Trust Me.* Then as I grappled with Him about what Hebrews 11:6 meant about His being a "rewarder," I sensed assurance of His all-sufficiency again with words from Genesis 15:1: "I am . . . your exceedingly great reward." Yet still I wrestled. *Which is more valuable to you?* God asked me. *Starting your marriage on a foundation of trust and faith in Me or a garden wedding and a foundation of financial security?*

This total consecration felt like too much. But God desires our faith to please Him, and when we seek Him with all our hearts, that truly is our greatest reward.

As God called Cliff and me into deeper faith and trust, we felt a nudging impression to give away all our wedding *ang bao*s to two anti–sex-trafficking ministries run by missionary friends of ours in Cambodia and India. When other friends heard about our plans, many cautioned us with wagging fingers, "Starting a marriage on a negative bank balance is very inauspicious!" And, "Well, at least save some for yourself. You don't have to give it all away!"

The night before our wedding, I got cold feet. Had we made a foolish decision?

Believe That God Is the Greatest Giver

Our ceremony took place in our home church, and the *ang bao* gifts amounted to more than fifty thousand dollars. That was enough to purchase two buildings to start factories giving employment to women rescued from red-light districts in Cambodia and India. I comforted myself with *This satisfaction of helping others is our reward.*

But God is not only a rewarder of faith; He's a Father of good gifts. He had more in store for us. And He remembered my dream.

Six months after our wedding, we received an email from Cliff's friends in Canada, where he was from. *Come back here for another wedding ceremony! We've pooled money to purchase flight tickets for you both!*

I'm sure my eyes were dazzling at God's rekindling of my dream of a garden wedding. I spent hours imagining a forest dripping with flowers, faultless iron-pressed tablecloths, and white wooden chairs. It would be perfect.

In a squall of emotion, I emailed two dozen possible wedding locations, sharing a link to the video testimony of how we met, filmed by a stranger who had heard of our unique love story and offered to film us for free.[2] Days passed, and my hopes dimmed as I scrolled through emailed replies like *Our wedding venues are typically booked a year in advance* and *Your budget is unworkable for us.*

I felt small and unimportant, desperate to receive news I could fall into with tumbling gratitude. But as reality set in, I trimmed my expectations.

"How about a barbecue in a friend's backyard?" one friend suggested.

My prayers pried open a door for fresh doubts. *God, is this dream of a garden wedding not from you? Is it too frivolous to earnestly seek you for it?* I no longer saw how my whimsical childhood request could fit into His grander, eternal purposes. Perhaps God didn't care about such things. I forgot, though, that His economy is different from ours. He has infinite provision, infinite time, infinite love. He can run the universe *and* hear our deepest heart cries. He can provide for the poor *and* provide for us. He can satisfy our basic needs *and* give good gifts.

He is God, and nothing is impossible for Him!

One day I received an email I never expected: *Here at Toronto Botanical Gardens, we receive hundreds of emails a day, but when I watched your video, I cried . . . I would very much like to help you.*

My jaw dropped open. Toronto Botanical Gardens is one of the world's top-ten wedding destinations. How could this be? Hebrews 11:6 flashed in my mind: "He is a rewarder of those who diligently seek Him." God's good gift definitely surpassed anything I'd dared to dream. For just over a thousand dollars, we were hosted in their newly launched gardens, dripping with flowers, complete with a large auditorium and elegant hors d'oeuvres. This was far more than the milk and brownies I'd imagined at a backyard barbecue!

The previous year people had warned us not to do the foolhardy thing, giving away our wedding *ang baos*. They reminded us of statistics, of how many marriages fail because of financial troubles. But God's supernatural ways supersede our human laws. When we give, He gives more. When we seek His righteousness first, He gives all that we need and more (Matthew 6:33).

What God is looking for is an all-out, radical faith that diligently seeks who He is and His goodness. He wants us to give our all, and Hebrews 11:6 reminds us His recompense is sure. While we gave away the fifty thousand dollars given to us at our initial wedding, I suspect the sponsorship by Toronto Botanical Gardens for our garden wedding exceeded that amount. Above all, we received a heavenly deposit of faith, set as a memorial stone in our lives, priceless.

Do not misunderstand. I'm not saying God will compensate us financially every time we give. I'm saying that God's economy is far different from what we imagine. The more we give, the more we will receive, even in ways we don't expect (Luke 6:38).

In our journey to pursue His dreams for our lives, God wants to use everyday experiences to strengthen our faith muscles. How else can we carry the spiritual load He has in store for us? Oh, how He desires to meet us in that deeply personal place to gift us with His goodness when we diligently seek Him in faith! Our obedience unlocks His faithfulness, our faith, His gifts.

But alas, another plot twist.

On our wedding day in Canada, dark clouds brooded. I closed my eyes to avoid the impending reality as lightning lit up the sky and then thunder rolled in the distance. In the garden, amid perfect white chairs, multicolored umbrellas sprouted like mushroom blooms. Rain like needles pelted down. Everyone made a beeline for the auditorium. And at exactly ten thirty, when the wedding procession should have begun outside, the skies unleashed their unrestrained fury.

I didn't even try to feign being cool. Backstage, I squatted in a corner like a crushed paper bag, a picture of inelegance in my pompous wedding gown, devastated. If God had taken the grand trouble to answer my prayer through this incredible series of divine miracles, then why this? It must be a bad joke. I felt the urge to call off the ceremony and make everyone reappear the next day when the sun would shine.

"No, no, no," I said over and over, shaking my head.

The sky and rain and ground merged into a silver sheet, thick and unyielding. I wrapped myself in a film of defiance, unwilling to accept this unreasonable outcome.

"Maybe we can wait it out?" said one of the groomsmen. But the rains gave way to whipping winds, and I glowered at him. My zeal to share my testimony of God's provision for this wedding ceremony evaporated. But then I felt stained with shame, for feeling angry with God. Still, this felt like a mockery, a testing of my faith in front of an audience on my special wedding day. What an uncanny conspiracy!

The bridal party watched me nervously. I heard the shuffle of shifting feet, of people unsure what to do, and waited to wake up from the nightmare. Cliff whisked in just in time for me to begin crying into his shoulder.

It never occurred to me to have a rain plan. Surely God would not have bent the world backward only to have the skies pour on us. Did He use up His powers so the last bit of meteorological execution failed to come through?

But then I heard, *Your circumstances don't give you reason to thank Me. Rather, your faith to trust in My goodness, no matter what the circumstances, is what truly glorifies Me.* Hebrews 11:6 came to mind again: "Without faith it is impossible to please Him, for he who comes to God must believe that He is, and that He is a rewarder of those who diligently seek Him." Despite my grave disappointment, did I have faith in God's goodness? Did I still trust He is a good Father with good gifts?

It finally dawned on me that as all eyes fell on me, I was given the greatest opportunity to glorify God, to declare that no matter what happens, He is a rewarder of faith and a good, good Father. After all, did He not grant us the amazing opportunity to have a second wedding ceremony with Canadian friends present? Wasn't that in itself a luxury?

As I walked toward Cliff down the aisle again, this time indoors and the rain still falling outside, I resolved that a downpour could not cloud out the magnificent goodness of God. In front of our friends and family, I took the microphone and said with smudged mascara, "I know this is awkward." Somber faces stared back at me. "But guess what! God is *still* good. And today I want to declare the truth He revealed to me as I walked down this aisle—that no matter what happens in our lives, we can have faith in His goodness. He is a good Father."

With theatrical drama, the rain abruptly stopped. Daylight streamed in through the windows, shimmering streams of gold. Pockets of sunshine pooled on the floor tiles, glowing with hope. Gingerly, I stepped aside to open the door and peek outside. A magical mist had descended upon the garden, aflame with color. The air, filled with the scent of sky and fruit, smelled light and sweet.

Then in front of the beautiful garden wedding setup, we once again sealed our vows and together laughed that truly "the third time's the charm."

Our photographer clicked away furiously, squealing like a schoolgirl with delight at the mystical afterglow created by the cloud cover. Pockets of sunshine appeared and disappeared mysteriously, luminously. "We are chasing the light!" she said. "This is amazing!

Then she told us, "I have a surprise for you."

She led us to a stable nearby and showed us a dream stallion, black and handsome and terrifying all at the same time. I teared up. "How did you know I love horses?"

Just as our photoshoot ended, the rain returned with a vengeance.

Believe Your Thanks Makes Way for the Miraculous

Friends, not all our dreams will have fairy-tale endings. Not all our cries, even if made in faith, will give us what we desire and expect. I sure wished it hadn't rained that day, but then I wouldn't be able to testify of God's goodness in this way.

If we choose to abide in faith, if we go to God believing in His goodness, shall we not discover that He is still a just rewarder of those who earnestly seek Him?

John 6:11 shows us how thanksgiving multiplies provision: "Jesus took the loaves, and when He had given thanks He distributed them to the disciples, and the disciples to those sitting down; and likewise of the fish, as much as they wanted." When we thank God for the miraculous, guess what! Our thanks opens a portal for the miraculous, for His goodness. When I opened my mouth to thank God for the wedding even when it rained, I believe my faith in His goodness pleased Him.

And lest we forget, the boy who gave up his five loaves and two fish gave up *all* he had. His willingness to offer his all for Jesus catalyzed a miracle that fed not only thousands of others but I'm sure him as well.

Today, if you're struggling to believe in God's goodness, know this: without faith, it's impossible to please God. But as we come to Him believing in His unchangeable attributes, that He is good no matter what our circumstances might be, and we willingly give up our all, our gratitude unlocks His Father's heart. When we trust that the rain in our lives doesn't change God's character and still willingly offer our all to Him, He rewards that simple faith.

My hope is that my wedding story has encouraged you to seek God's kingdom first, above all else, and to take those aching longings in your heart to Abba Father. My prayer is that you'll then see the mercies, goodness, and love of a God whose character is unchanging and true with a heart warmed by gratitude.

May the Lord grant you His grace to give your all to Him, to trust and obey Him, and in living out His dreams for you, to witness the unthinkable rewards of His endlessly lavish, extravagant love.

FOR REFLECTION

1. What does seeking first God's kingdom and His righteousness look like for you?
2. What holds you back from doing this?
3. How does knowing that God is a "rewarder of those who diligently seek Him" encourage you to apply faith in your situation?

NEXT STEPS

1. Write down one thing God is calling you to surrender to Him to put His kingdom first.
2. List what you would lose by obeying God. Take time to grieve that loss and share your pain with Him.
3. Write a personal prayer of thanksgiving to thank God for your circumstances, no matter what they might be. Then declare your thanks aloud.

PRAYER

God, you know where I struggle to put your kingdom first. Grant me the kind of faith that pleases you, that trusts in your goodness. When I think about all I need to give up to follow your requests, my heart wavers. Hold me in your arms as I grieve my losses. Will you help me experience your extravagant love as the Father of good gifts and rewarder of faith? Help me trust that your rewards are worth infinitely more than my sacrifices. Let me be a witness to a series of your miraculous ways as I give my all to you, even as I give my dreams back to you. I love you, Abba Father. Amen.

6

make the more excellent sacrifice

> By faith Abel offered to God a more excellent sacrifice than Cain, through which he obtained witness that he was righteous, God testifying of his gifts; and through it he being dead still speaks.
>
> —Hebrews 11:4

ONE DAY, after he'd asked us to see him, Cliff and I made an appointment to visit our senior pastor in his office. When we did, his voice, usually filled with such zeal over the pulpit, boomed in the little room.

"As you know, we have a church plant in Uganda, and the local pastor needs help. You both would be a great blessing there."

We'd always said we were open to missional work wherever God called us, but now my heart shuddered with the first of many challenges that came into my head. "U-Uganda?" I stammered.

"Yes.

"But you-you see, we know the yellow fever vaccine is a mandatory requirement for entry to Uganda. Cliff has a liver transplant, and he can't take that vaccine."

Just before we married, Cliff suffered an unexplainable but serious liver crisis episode. As I told you earlier, his liver enzyme markers had skyrocketed and alarmed his specialists enough for them to order a biopsy to investigate the possibility of cancer recurrence, and my parents were more concerned about his health than anything else.

The anxiety I felt now had plagued me then as well. My worry of losing him drained life of its color. One moment I would be enjoying dinner with Cliff at our favorite restaurant, and the next I would imagine how unthinkable it would be for me to return to the same place if he passed on.

Our pastor looked me in the eye. "Will you trust God for this?"

Was he implying my faith in God had worn thin? How could that be fair?

As soon as we left our pastor's office, Cliff asked me point-blank, "Are you willing to say yes?"

Say yes? How could he think it so simple? How could I say yes to potentially losing him to a completely preventable illness?

One night I awoke, breathing hard, my chest heaving in and out like a metal cage. My heart took on a life of its own, fleeing from the horror of possibly losing Cliff. The turmoil closed in on me, and I felt suffocated. While I'd had no control over my husband's bizarre liver crisis episode before we married, I had some control over his health now. I could refuse such an assignment. Yet that quiet voice I'd come to know asked, *Will you put your faith in Me?* The question whirred up a hurricane within me, tearing up my inner anchors of security.

"God," I prayed aloud, choking on tears as Cliff tried to soothe me back to sleep, "if Uganda is where you want us to go, give me the faith to obey you."

During the day, distraction cushioned my mind. But at night my thoughts unraveled like yarn and my body felt tight with foreboding. At a recent Christian gathering, a missionary had shared about losing his ten-year-old daughter from a completely preventable illness while serving in the field. My heart quivered as he spoke. Scenes of me resuscitating Cliff in the field and struggling to evacuate him flashed in my mind.

Sometimes I'd open our wardrobe to pick out a shirt for him, only to be hijacked by thoughts of his passing, a whole rack of shirts looking back at me as I speculated on a future misery. I knew it wasn't normal to live like this, but being faced with that real possibility so early in our marriage traumatized me. Anxiety, like cobwebs, filled the attics of my mind.

Didn't our pastor understand the gravity of the matter? That I'd already thought I might lose Cliff once? That this risk was real? How about all the unreached people groups in Asia? Hardly any of those countries required a vaccine Cliff couldn't take.

I can't say yes. Help me, Lord. Give me a way out.

I must tell you this.

One day when I was alone, tears streaming down my cheeks, I came face-to-face with my heart's deceit. This wasn't just about Cliff's health. Something else was at play.

While part of me loved Jesus to the point of sacrificial living, another part of me loved the success my life attracted. I was pursuing the glamorous path of becoming a surgeon, and I was midway in my application for further studies at Johns Hopkins to earn a Master of Public Health. I loved my life.

And contrary to what you might think, though Cliff and I had experienced a stirring in our hearts to go further, go lower, go deeper, persistently nudging us toward missional work as a couple, neither of us had experienced a dramatic *Lord, send us!* moment.

So what about my career and further studies? Wasn't God asking too much from me? Could I really follow through on sacrificially serving the poor—even for just a year with so much at stake? We'd even have to give up our new home. And Cliff's health was still my main concern.

The missionary dream God had planted in me when I was eighteen years old flickered like a candle's flame in the wind, fragile and faint. During the day, I avoided the office break room, fearful of the searing comments and questions. At night, I struggled, weeping myself to sleep.

Hebrews 11:4 says, "By faith Abel offered to God a more excellent sacrifice than Cain, through which he obtained witness that he was righteous, God testifying of his gifts; and through it he being dead still speaks." This verse states how Abel's sacrifice appeared "more excellent" to God because he had given it "by faith." Genesis 4:4–5 states, "The Lord respected Abel and his offering, but He did not respect Cain and his offering." In the Hebrew language, the words *had respect to* translate into "kindle into a fire," suggesting that Abel's offering, being consumed by fire, marked God's divine approval (Genesis 15:17).[1]

What was it about Abel's offering that made it more excellent? Genesis 4:4 states, "Abel also brought of the firstborn of his flock and of their fat." Above what Cain had brought, a mere thank offering, in faith Abel felt his need of a propitiatory sacrifice to atone for his sins. Thus it was faith that caused Abel's offering to please God. Lest we think it was the intrinsic merit in "the firstling of the flock" above "the fruit of the ground" that pleased God; this is not true.[2] If so, it would have been a presumptuous act of will-worship (Colossians 2:23). Rather, it was Abel's faith manifested in the sin offering that pleased God.[3]

In pursuing God's dreams for our lives, God requires us to make sacrifices. Will we make sacrifices truly acceptable in His sight, or only those that make Him lament (1 Samuel 15:22)?

As I continue my story about our call to Uganda, I hope you'll be encouraged to give God the "more excellent sacrifice" He asks for through obedience to and faith in Him.

Be Willing to Lay It All Down

I visited a missionary friend for advice about Cliff's health, hoping for some words of inspiration. Instead, he matter-of-factly said, "It would be medically irresponsible of you to allow Cliff to serve in Africa with his condition."

Desperate, I offered God alternatives. Surely I could give Him a different sacrifice that sat well with both Him and me?

One morning I emailed an infectious disease professor from medical school. I thought he would advise us conservatively. With his medical advice against our travel to Uganda, I could decline my pastor's suggestion. Instead, he referred me to a travel medicine subspecialist. *See me at my travel clinic with Cliff's health records,* her email read.

Cliff and I both went, and as she sifted through his formidable mound of health records, I nodded to her quiet exclamation, "Wow, this is quite remarkable." *So she can see how complicated Cliff's case is, how unwise it would be for us to go,* I thought.

But when her head emerged from the pile, her face erupting into a Cheshire smile, she said, "You're in the right place! I contributed to the World Health Organization guidelines for the yellow fever vaccine, and based on your condition, Cliff, and the current risks in the area you'd be flying to, I feel God's peace over writing you an official waiver letter so you can go to Uganda *without* that vaccination."

Cliff beamed with delight while I went into quiet hysteria, unsure of whether to pound the floor or implode inward.

"You prayed for God to show you," Cliff reminded me.

My well-laid plans to seek firm medical advice against going to Uganda or at least to negotiate a different location had been thwarted. I wanted to escape, but God had led us right back into His hands.

"You guys are so fortunate," the subspecialist said sprightly, oblivious to my shock. "I'm usually *never* in Singapore this time of year."

Excitedly, Cliff booked air tickets for a short ten-day reconnaissance trip to Uganda.

Nothing prepared us for how beautiful Uganda is. Its vast lands and endless waters swallowed us into its raw grandeur, and the country welcomed us with open arms.

One thing on our itinerary distracted me, though—a visit to the city hospital. I'd set one goal for myself: find a hepatologist to care for Cliff. *God, if this is where you want us, will you grant me grace? Will you provide a hepatologist for Cliff to assure me you'll look after him?*

At the entrance, my eyes scanned the large whiteboard with red scribblings listing the hospital's various departments. Then my heart sank.

"Is there no hepatology department here?" I asked the receptionist.

"No, I'm *so* sorry." She exuded what I came to know as the typical hospitable Ugandan glow with its characteristic apologetic tone.

Visitors milled around while healthcare staff scurried past us. I felt helpless at the mercy of a foreign hospital system. If something happened to Cliff, what would I do?

God, how could you leave me alone with this burden to bear? My worries madly swam inside me. But Cliff looked stoic. He was all ready to die for the Lord at any cost, at any time.

I hung my head low. After already falling madly in love with Uganda, this felt like a blow to my face, a betrayal of some sort.

As we walked out of the hospital, a handsome-looking man with ebony skin glistening against his white coat towered over us. "You are *lost,*" he said, emphasizing his last word, Ugandan-speak for "May I help you?"

Cliff let me answer, and I explained his condition halfheartedly. What did it matter? This conversation wouldn't change the fact that there didn't seem to be anyone to provide the specialized care Cliff needed.

Reaching into his coat's pocket, the man handed me a card and then said to me, "Ma'am, I'm the medical director of this hospital. This is my personal number. If your husband here ever needs medical attention, please call me directly. I'm available for you 24/7 and will personally see to his care and, if necessary, evacuation."

A wave of emotion swept over me, and I felt God's love hold me tightly so I wouldn't fall on the red dirt. At once, the cords of fear and anxiety that bound me broke open. Goose bumps tingled all over as I felt God's warm presence. I knew this was not coincidence but His divine orchestration. I heard His gentle whisper, *Can you love Cliff more than I do?*

I'd suffered recurrent nightmares and panic attacks about losing Cliff to illness, jolting upright in the night, my hands wildly gripping his, my heart pounding like the hooves of fierce horses. An unbroken string of haunting visions had vandalized my mind. But that day healed me forever. I never suffered a single panic attack about losing him again.

That evening, I heard God tenderly whisper, *You may be Cliff's wife, but My love for him is greater than yours. You may be a doctor, but My provision for his health is far greater than what you can ever offer. Are you ready to put your faith in Me?*

The heavy burden I'd carried for too long lifted. God showed me that, despite my poor view of Him, He loves us far more than I imagined. Despite unknowns ahead, He goes before us.

By the way, today Cliff is the healthiest he's ever been. His medication dosage has been quartered, and God has blessed us with a hepatologist who's always waived his consultation fees. He also came in fourth place in the most recent World Transplant Games in the triathlon category.

Count the Cost

Today, God is looking for men and women who will pay the price and give Him "the more excellent sacrifice" in faith in order to carry His promises to reality. He's looking for people not just willing to give up what is convenient or easy to surrender but also willing to repent of their sins, lay down their all, and yield to His will. Most of all, He's waiting for lovers of Himself to commit themselves so fully to the fruition of His dreams for them that they will, at any cost and like Abel, sacrifice all and leave a legacy of faith (Hebrews 11:4).

You may have received prophecies about God's dreams for your life but never acted on them because they seemed too costly. Some of these dreams require major life adjustments, like changing your job, settling for a smaller paycheck, or selling your home. They may require that you, like me, count the cost of losing someone you love. Yet in Matthew 10:37–39, God tells us, "He who loves father or mother more than Me is not worthy of Me. . . . And he who does not take his cross and follow after Me is not worthy of Me. He who finds his life will lose it, and he who loses his life for My sake will find it."

Do you have real concerns about forsaking your all to pursue God's call, His dream, for your life? Does it seem too hard to say yes? When I put our two lives into His hands with wholehearted abandonment, I learned He would prove the radical surrender was worth it. For if He looks after the sparrows of the air and the grass of the fields and counts the number of hairs on our heads, can't He look after all our needs too?

The truth is if we choose to say no to His call, God will choose others. But the fact that He has stirred an unrest in your heart, that He's planted a dream, shows that He's calling *you*.

The key question is, Do you trust His plans are better than yours, even when you can't see the big picture? Do you trust He will lead you to a good place because of His lavish love? Most of us need the assurance of a better plan before we can ditch our current one. Yet God often requires us to take the first step of faith before He reveals the next step to us. Most of us want to weigh the cost of our sacrifice. Yet when the angel appeared to Mary to share God's plans for her and said, "The power of the Highest will overshadow you" (Luke 1:35), she didn't negotiate. She said, "Let it be to me according to your word" (verse 38).

No matter how impossible God's promises may seem to you, we can respond the way Mary did if we trust God with all our hearts. Like Abel, we can, by faith in God's goodness, give Him our "more excellent sacrifice."

God is calling. Despite your fears and anxieties about walking into His will, will you put them aside and trust Him?

I hope you will choose courage. I hope you will dream brave. Count the cost and choose faith. Choose to give God your more excellent sacrifice, always. Because it will always be worth it.

FOR REFLECTION

1. In your journey to fulfilling God's dreams in your life, what kinds of sacrifices is God calling you to make?
2. What have you been bargaining or negotiating with God about?
3. What would "counting the cost" look like in your current situation?

NEXT STEPS

1. List sacrifices you know you'll have to make in your journey to pursue God's dreams for your life.
2. In a chart like this one, write down fears you have. Then write in some Bible verses that would help you overcome those fears when they attack you. You may take inspiration from the examples given.

Fears I have:	Verses that will give me courage:
I fear losing my income and all the comforts it could buy.	My God will supply every need of yours according to his riches in glory in Christ Jesus (Philippians 4:19 ESV)

3. Write a make-believe obituary for yourself. What do you think people will say about your faith when you die?

PRAYER

God, I know the sacrifices I need to make to follow your call for my life, to dream brave. Yet I try to bargain with you. And at times, it's easier to give you a more convenient sacrifice. Will you help me yield to your will, even after I've counted the cost? Give me courage to overcome my fears. Help me, like Abel did, give you the "more excellent sacrifice." Help me, like Mary did, give you my wholehearted yes. Amen.

7

persevere when your faith is under fire

> Others were tortured, not accepting deliverance, that they might obtain a better resurrection. Still others had trial of mockings and scourgings, yes, and of chains and imprisonment.
>
> —Hebrews 11:35–36

How could you do this? It's dangerous in Uganda."

"What about your futures? Your finances? Your residency? Your house?"

"Haven't you considered Cliff's health?"

"How must your parents feel?"

"You're approaching the peak of your medical career. If you leave now, you'll regret it."

Once we gingerly opened the door for conversation about our journey to Uganda, questions pelted us and grew with vigor and ferocity. They pounded us incessantly, thunderously, and would not let up even when we shut the door tightly behind us. Questions we didn't yet have answers to and questions we never thought of left us wordless, anxious.

When Jesus said to follow Him, I'm sure He didn't mean this! I thought to myself one day.

Why did this feel so hard? I felt like I was being persecuted for my faith while stepping toward the dream God had put in our hearts—to serve the poor wherever He called us. An incredible loneliness set in. It was one thing to explain our decision to those without a faith in God, but even Christians thought we were crazy.

Hebrews 11:35–36 says, "Others were tortured, not accepting deliverance, that they might obtain a better resurrection. Still others had trial of mockings and scourgings, yes, and of chains and imprisonment."

The word *tortured* here is derived from the Greek τύμπανον, describing how the sufferer, stretched on an instrument like a drumhead, was "broken on a wheel" and scourged to death. Body bent, the victim's pain worsened as lashes cut deeper on an extended body, exposing flesh to open air. Verses 37 and 38 reveal the suffering of martyrs—being stoned, sawn, slain, and made homeless. Despite this, though, they chose not to renounce their opinions or faith to gain life. Why? Because they looked forward to a more honorable, more lasting restoration to life in a heavenly realm.[1]

In our journeys to obey God, not all of us will be persecuted through scourging. Cliff and I certainly haven't. Yet the mockery from a watching world can be painful, torturous even. As we carry our crosses for God in obedience, we may endure what the world deems "needless suffering." Make no mistake, if you choose to live counterculturally, your choices for God will invite taunts. You might feel like you're being put through a furnace. But will you choose to allow the heat in those situations to refine you in the crucible of faith? Or, bent by the lashings from human tongues, will you give up?

As God was faithful to the martyrs of old, these verses in Hebrews 11 encourage us to trust God and hold on to His promises despite our sufferings. As the martyrs of faith endured, so can we.

How we must persevere when our faith comes under fire! When we willingly choose to embrace suffering on the path of obedience for the sake of a "better resurrection," our hardships and heartbreaks are never wasted. Our faith merely comes forth as gold.

To encourage you to remain steadfast in hard times, I'd like to share a challenging experience we encountered in Uganda.

Soon after we made our decision, we left our first home. I was now twenty-six years old, and little did I know this would be only the first of a dozen goodbyes we would make to homes, places, and people in the years to come.

Our year in Uganda was phenomenal. We held hands and broke bread with broken people. We prayed and travailed for breakthrough with people under tin roofs and inside mud walls. We walked and grieved with people who loved and lost. We sowed with tears, and we reaped in joy.

But some days were hard. Cliff and I lived in a little clinic-turned-living-quarters at the top of a hill within an HIV health center. Our bed was a mattress on the floor, and we slept under a mosquito net, its holes patched with tape. When it rained, water seeped in through the window louvres and under the doors. On many a monsoon night, we scrambled out of bed to soak up water in the flooding room with towels. Occasionally, we were bitten by jungle insects that left our flesh swollen and hot for days. On days that were scorching hot, we would return from the village desperate for a shower only to find the water supply cut. On our wedding anniversary, after I'd prepared all the ingredients to cook an elaborate surprise meal for Cliff, the power went out.

One night as we were about to sleep, we felt the ground shake.

"What's that?" I asked.

Boom. Boom! Boom. Boom!

"I think it's music," Cliff said.

"At this time of night?"

A street-bar disco that blasted music every other night made its presence known for miles. The techno beats started at ten, then crescendoed throughout the night before the grand finale at five in the morning. Bleary eyed, Cliff and I would pray for it to stop. But it never did.

When we wrote and shared our struggles, people wrote back, *Why don't you guys come home?* The temptation was real. After all, wasn't serving under these conditions for a few months enough of a sacrifice? The world raced and climbed ahead while we struggled with daily living. Perhaps we'd made the wrong choice. Perhaps the sacrifice just wasn't worth it.

Another morning at 2 a.m., psychotic laughing jerked us into wide-eyed vigilance. Sound traveled boldly through the roof we shared with the health center and open louvres, echoing eerily against the metal pipes. Wooden doors slammed, and metal bowls clanged. Serrated howls punctured the night like nails on a steel pole.

I wrapped myself in a cloak that billowed wildly in the whipping winds as we went outside to discover what was going on. Unbeknownst to us, the HIV health center had converted the rooms next to ours into a full-blown hospital ward. For months we'd tried to adjust to these various disturbances. Weren't we promised a quiet residence? This was too much. I looked at my husband. Hollows had appeared under his eyes, his skin dark and sunken from sleepless nights.

"Wai Jia . . ." He paused for effect. "You have to expect hardship in your journey to obedience."

"But I want to go back to Singapore! I'm through with this!"

"You can, Wai Jia," he said calmly. "You have a choice."

The next morning, worn out, I sank into a corner of the kitchen floor and bawled. *Is this what I gave up pursuing a career in surgery for?*

Voices in my head taunted me. *Well, you said you wanted this.*

Then I felt God's gentle embrace, and I sensed Him telling me, *There is life beyond all this pain*. Matthew 13:45–46 came to mind: "The kingdom of heaven is like a merchant seeking beautiful pearls, who, when he had found one pearl of great price, went and sold all that he had and bought it."

I marveled at this. Did the merchant, who owned great riches, really sell "all he had" for the pearl? How great his trust in its worth must have been! In contrast, the rich young ruler in Mark 10:21–22, whom Jesus told, "Sell whatever you have and give to the poor, and you will have treasure in heaven; and come, take up the cross, and follow Me," was "sad at this word, and went away sorrowful, for he had great possessions."

No one had broken my body on a drum. No one had asked me to sell everything I owned. Yet as I sat on that kitchen floor in a puddle of tears, I felt stretched beyond measure.

"When will you bring me relief, God?" I cried aloud. "When can we leave this place and head back home?"

God's gentle whisper answered me: *Will you allow these pains to press you closer to Me? Or will you allow them to drive you away, like the rich young ruler did? For the pearl of great price, for the price of knowing Me, for a better resurrection, do you dare forsake everything to serve Me?*

Did I truly believe His pearl was worth my all?

Suffering Is Never Wasted

I'm aware that sometimes people look at Cliff and me as though we're heroic. They think we must be different. But we're not. I like drinking perfectly foamed lattes in hipster cafés, and I dream of perfect beach holidays. I like clean restrooms and immaculate, predictable schedules. I've held back tears at social occasions where my colleagues talked about their promotions, big paychecks, new cars, and exotic holidays. My faith wavers when it should not.

Yet the pain in our journey of obedience humbles us to know we are human, merely vessels for God's use. Our joint fellowship of His sufferings brings us comfort (Philippians 3:10). When we willingly choose to embrace suffering on the path of obedience, our tears and pain, hardships and heartbreaks, are never wasted.

At every step of the way, Jesus uses the grit of service and the pain of surrender to produce a pearl of character in our hearts. Like an oyster meeting a foreign irritant, our natural reaction may be to purge what vexes us and choose comfort. But it's precisely through the process of agonizing discomfort that God forms pearls for Himself. Like an oyster secreting a lacquer-like substance called nacre to coat the irritant, our choice to clothe ourselves in Christ's righteousness and truths in response to offenses, hardships, and affliction can result in a beautiful pearl of glory for Christ (Isaiah 61:10).

And the very thing we think will hinder our fulfillment of God's promises can be the very thing that propels us forward toward it.

One morning, after bearing with our increasingly difficult housing situation for months, the housing manager finally agreed to meet us. My heart dipped when I heard his preamble, said in a put-on American accent reserved for speaking with *mzungus* (foreigners), placating and patronizing.

"I have a myriad of options for you to choose from," he said. "You can stay put or move out."

A myriad?

"Those aren't really options," Cliff said dryly.

"Of course they are options," the man said with a chortle. "You are our *customers*, and we just want to make you happy."

I sat back, feeling assailed. Since when were we customers? Were we not volunteers who deserved a bit of appreciation for all we had done? Why did he infringe our housing agreement? I stewed inside, my self-righteousness bubbling up.

Then with dramatic pizzazz, the housing manager brought the watch on his left wrist to his face. "Ahh, I need to beat the rush-hour traffic home."

He left hurriedly, briefcase in hand.

As we sat on our front porch, I said to Cliff with mock wonder, "Wow, I guess this is it. Even if we move out, there's no guarantee the new place will be better. It's a continuum of discomfort we have to choose from."

Cliff burst out laughing. "My dear, our whole earthly life is a continuum of discomfort!"

Our hands clasped together, in part hope and part desperation.

A flood of messages gushed in from our prayer supporters after we shared the latest with them.

You guys need to get out immediately.

Don't see the option of moving out as failure.

You can always come back home.

I wondered aloud when this torture would end, and Cliff said, "God's in control, Wai Jia. Just wait and see."

As we prayed, we felt the Holy Spirit say, *Your painful prison experiences are fertile ground for precious lessons. If you try to jump out of them yourselves, you'll miss the chance for Me to refine you.* Then we had an inexplicable, puzzling peace that as long as we could tolerate the uncertainty of what tomorrow would bring, God would prove the certainty of His mercy and reality.

One morning at 4 a.m., huddled under the safety of a new mosquito net, I sensed God's gentle whisper asking me to release my rights, forgive the housing manager, and allow God Himself to vindicate us. The lion in me wanted to retaliate, fight for our rights, and demand fair recompense. Yet the familiar image of God as simultaneously a strong Lion and a meek Lamb reminded me of how even the King of all kings had suffered the gravest injustice with a spirit of meekness. At the end, it wasn't Christ who fought for His own rights but His Father who vindicated Him and restored Him to the throne.

Likewise, when persecuted, do we want to save ourselves? Or persevere amid trials and allow God to give us His better resurrection?

The same morning I surrendered my rights to God, the executive director of the HIV center asked to meet Cliff and me before her entire board of directors. "On behalf of our entire organization," she said there, "we want to apologize officially for our oversight. We are committed to making drastic changes to improve your living conditions at no cost to you."

Within days, a team of muscular, lanky men built a tall rattan fence between the clinic areas and our home for our privacy. They cemented the opening at the top of our walls and doorway to prevent noise from bouncing down the corridor from the patients to where we slept. They installed rubber stoppers to prevent the wooden doors from slamming. They posted daytime visiting hours and curfews for visitors who came in the evening.

God fought for us, and in the end, Jesus turned all our tears to joy when we saw hearts restored and lives changed. We would not have had it any other way.

In Philippians 3:7–11, the apostle Paul encourages us to count our earthly gains as losses "for the excellence of the knowledge of Christ Jesus" and to suffer for our losses for knowing "Him and the power of His resurrection, and the fellowship of His sufferings, being conformed to His death," so we may "attain to the resurrection from the dead." In this passage lies a common theme: the willingness to endure hardship for an unseen eternal reward.

In your quest to obey God and His call, are you afraid of encountering pain and persecution? You're not alone. In fact, so real was Jesus' fear of pain on the way to Calvary that He said to God, "Father, if it is Your will, take this cup away from Me." Yet His wholehearted trust and perfect obedience completed His sentence in the same breath: "Nevertheless not My will, but Yours, be done" (Luke 22:42).

When persecuted, Jesus persevered. When His faith came under fire, He surrendered His will to the Father's. In the same way, as we crucify our fears, anxieties, and aversion to pain by fixing our eyes on completing His will, God's grace will always be enough to see us through.

Friend, let's persevere when our faith comes under fire. May the fiery trials of our lives only refine us further. May we always come forth as gold.

FOR REFLECTION

1. What kinds of fiery trials (for example, mockery, taunting, rejection) have you experienced in saying yes to God's call?
2. How did it make you feel?
3. List some ways you cope with these challenges.

NEXT STEPS

1. List three Bible verses that will encourage you to persevere when times of hardship and persecution come. An example is James 1:12: "Blessed is the one who perseveres under trial because, having stood the test, that person will receive the crown of life that the Lord has promised to those who love him" (NIV).
2. List the names of people who may have persecuted or hurt you and whom you wish to forgive.
3. Write down merits of your character development when you've endured trials.

PRAYER

God, thank you for the Bible's martyrs whose enduring faith and trust in you shine as examples for us still today. I acknowl-

edge how the pains you allow in my life press me closer to you. Give me perseverance under persecution when my faith is under fire. Grant me the confidence of a better eternal reward, a better resurrection, that my faith comes out pure as gold at the very end. In Jesus' name I pray, amen.

8

wait on God and his promises

> All these, having obtained a good testimony through faith, did not receive the promise, God having provided something better for us, that they should not be made perfect apart from us.
>
> —Hebrews 11:39–40

YOU AND ME, Dr. Wai, hand in hand. We can do this!"

"Yes, Miremba. But take it easy, okay? You'll need time to recuperate."

In her last month of carrying her fourth child, Miremba needed rest. But witnessing her passion and commitment in improving geriatric care for the vulnerable elderly in Uganda inspired me to plow on too. Together, we closely worked toward a vision of every elderly person being cared for in their communities.

"Don't worry. I'm going to take a nice rest over the weekend in my village," she told me. "You and I make a great team! We're going to change the healthcare landscape for the elderly in Uganda. See you next week."

That was the last thing she said to me. The following Monday, word of her death came round.

"What? What do you mean Miremba died?" I stood with feet frozen.

"She died in childbirth over the weekend."

"No, we're meeting today. We're discussing the plans for elderly advocacy."

"She went into early labor, Dr. Wai. She over-bled. The funeral is tomorrow."

I sat down to steady myself.

The days that followed heaved with aching pain. I awoke in the morning, plagued with guilt, and with Miremba gone, a hole grew in my heart. *Why, God, why?*

Miremba's death meant the loss of a friend. But it also meant the death of a work we'd started together.

"I am sorry, but we can't find a replacement," the director of the health center told me.

Miremba had networks and connections no one else in the health center had. No one could access her computer. She knew things about future partnerships and plans that I was only just beginning to learn. All my hard work died along with her.

Despite all my obedience and sacrifice, my service felt like emptying the sea with a teaspoon. Why did we come? What was the point of God sending us to Uganda when He knew my work would be flushed?

I couldn't see a future in the work, and I stared blankly at my half-empty glass.

Hebrews 11:39–40 says, "All these [patriarchs], having obtained a good testimony through faith, did not receive the promise, God having provided something better for us, that they should not be made perfect apart from us." The words *having obtained a good testimony* find their root in the Greek word μαρτυρέω, which means to "bear witness" or "give evidence." What was the promise the patriarchs in Hebrews 11, who bore witness and held evidence of faith in God, did not enjoy in their lifetime?

Romans 8:1–4 gives us a glimpse of what "something better" refers to—what we now enjoy, a life with Christ, free from the law of sin and death, a life unavailable to the old patriarchs of faith. Yet there's more. God is also preparing a city in eternity for us all and promises us the *final completion* of "salvation" at Christ's coming again (Hebrews 9:28, 11:10). Hebrews 11:40 encourages us that all who trust in God will be "made perfect" and transformed together. Therefore, the patriarchs of old and we may enjoy the same privileges, "that they should not be made perfect apart from us."[1]

These verses remind us that those with true faith hold steadfast to God even when they don't receive His promises immediately. They do so because they trust God's plans from His eternal perspective. They trust that He has "something better" in store for them.

In our journeys to follow God's call for our lives, we'll likely experience disappointment. The fullness of the vision He gave to us may seem so far away. You might be a struggling entrepreneur with a bleeding monthly expenditure, a parent wrestling with a wayward teenager, or a leader grappling with a floundering ministry. Amid life's disappointments, it might feel like all your efforts will amount to nothing. Yet having witnessed the evidence of God's faith working in your life, and having received a glimpse of His promises, will you continue to press on and wait on God for eternal rewards you cannot yet see?

That is what Hebrews 11:39–40 is all about.

In this chapter I share a peculiar incident in Uganda I hope will inspire you toward a more confident faith. Even when all our efforts seem to be going down the drain, may we eagerly await the fulfillment of God's promises—even if it may happen beyond our lifetime.

The Ingredients for a Miracle

One Sunday, Dembe, the wife of our Ugandan friend Akello, came to me sheepishly while begging her husband to translate as she recounted a dream for me. Her Luganda-language words had a teasing lilt, but her serious tone birthed butterflies in my gut.

"I dreamt I was pregnant and lost my baby. It slipped out of me, and the doctors could not save it. Then suddenly, I saw you, Dr. Wai, and a man. His face was so white and so bright that I couldn't see it. He stood behind you. Together, you put my baby back into me. Then my baby lived."

Goose bumps crawled up the back of my arms.

Months later, Akello approached us. "Pastor Cliff! Dr. Wai! Please pray against this terrible witchcraft!"

"What's wrong?"

"Dembe is being attacked by vicious spirits. When she tries to lie down, there is a fire in her belly! In the day, the spirits torment her with vomiting."

I asked gently, "Have you tested if she's pregnant?"

True enough, Dembe was expecting.

Months later, Akello called to say, "Dr. Wai! Pastor Cliff! Please pray for my wife. She's going to deliver prematurely." Anxious, we prayed together, then heaved a collective sigh of relief when his baby was born. Later he called to say, "Pray for us! Dembe's going into the operating theater now." I quivered with anxiety. Did her dream mean I had some role to play?

Nothing brought me more relief than when I held the tiny newborn in my arms. "She is beautiful," I said, looking into a face of perfect peace.

"We named her Divine."

Finally, I can put the troubling dream aside, I thought. *It's over.*

The next day we visited the couple in a spartan brick building atop a balding hill, befittingly named Grade B Hospital. Dembe lay on a metal trolley with no mattress. I looked around. Few if any health workers could be seen, and most rooms stood empty. Bereft of funds, beds, and medical equipment, the hospital was starved of care.

The next morning, however, took a sharp turn. Baby Divine's skin had turned a worrying blue. Without any neonatology facilities at Grade B Hospital, Akello panicked and called us. "My baby is going to die. What's your advice, Dr. Wai? Help us, please!" His voice trembled. I could see him pacing, frantic. The shaky timbre in his voice made my fingers cold at the tips.

My heart leaked empty. "I'm sorry. I'm not a baby doctor. There's nothing I can do." My paltry words flopped like cream cake on gravel. "But we will pray for you."

"What? Oh, I see . . ." Now his voice was heavy with despair, and this time my heart broke.

When I sank into a chair on our front porch, a puddle of self-pity formed around me. Surely I could do more. In my mind I saw Akello pacing back and forth like a metronome, up and down the corridors, pulling at health workers for help while his baby's life hung by a thread.

My fingers went into a frenzy of action. I texted senior pediatric colleagues from Singapore, asking for help. But it was useless. Nothing they advised could be done in a hospital with no facilities.

Restless, I began to pace as if I could walk away from the situation. Tears pushed out of my eyes as I recalled an African doctor's recent words to me: "You should have waited to come when you had more qualifications." The voice echoed hauntingly, and I buried my head in my hands.

"Surely Dembe's dream means something," Cliff whispered. "I don't know how, but surely you have a part to play in this."

Dembe's dream flooded my mind, and something within me heaved and ebbed like a stirring tempest, refusing to be quelled. "Pray with me, Cliff."

As I stilled my soul in God, I heard His voice: *When have I asked you to give what you do not have?*

In the valley of desperate prayer, I remembered the humble ingredients needed for a miracle—five loaves and two fish, the widow's oil and her neighbor's earthen jars, water before it turned into wine. What God really wants from us is simply hearts of yieldingness, ready to let Him multiply the little we can offer. *I love to use ordinary, broken people. I love to turn ashes into beauty.* As I heard His voice, the sagging moon-weight in my heart lifted. I gasped for relief as if emerging from under water.

Then I remembered the twelve basketsful of leftovers. The jars filled with oil, the widow's debt paid. I remembered the six stone water jars, each holding twenty to thirty gallons, all filled to the brim with choice wine. And suddenly I understood. The greater the needs around us, the more God is able to do. Our faith in Him can replace our deepest fears. He provides for all our needs and more. I knew I was not alone.

Pushed to press in, I cried aloud, "God, then show me what to do!"

The fog in my mind cleared, and even in my unbelief I knew He was turning water into wine. Even when I couldn't see the future. A calm clarity returned, and I walked to the health center and spoke with the pharmacist.

"Hi. I'm Dr. Wai living next door. Do you know how I can get an ambulance from Grade B Hospital to the National Referral Hospital in Kampala?"

My own words stunned me. Where did this idea come from? But I knew the Holy Spirit had planted it.

"We have ambulances," the pharmacist said, shaking his head in the characteristic Ugandan way, "but ah-ah, they have no oxygen tank. You can try Emmanuel Medical Centre. Call them?"

I sprang into action. Five calls later, I finally found the right person. "I need mobile money," said the gruff voice. "No mobile money, no rent ambulance."

Mobile money? What was that? Cliff and I jumped into our twenty-year-old tin car and sped down to a little phone kiosk. The car rattled, shaking with every rise and fall of the bumpy slope down the hill. Then—ah-ha!—we revved toward a wooden sign with the words *Mobile Money* hand-painted in blue.

"Ah-ah, today no credit here, ma'am. Over there," the man in the shack said as he pointed. "You go there."

Amid heavy traffic, we pulled over, parked, and sprinted to another shack across the road. A stout matron shook her head, then referred us to yet another shack, this one down the road. Like headless chickens, we darted from one shack to the next, desperate to find "mobile money" to help us with hiring an ambulance. Red dust sailed as we ran.

Finally, we did it! "See, so easy, ma'am. Money transfer over phone, so easy!"

With a wry laugh, we heaved a portentous sigh of relief.

Minutes later, an ambulance screeched past our home. With the money finally wired and the ambulance hired, Akello, Dembe, and their baby were whooshed to the National Referral Hospital down in the city of Kampala.

The next day, we visited the hospital there, a sprawling monstrosity of wards. Throngs of people blended into one another—traditional village wear into skirt-wraps, skirt-wraps into trousers, trousers into shirts, and shirts into picnic mats, all spread across the corridors as visitors ate, napped, and chatted on them.

Right at the edge of the maddening crowd, we saw baby Divine, her eyes closed, in a phototherapy box, totally weaned off oxygen.

"I don't know how to thank you," said Akello, his white smile breaking his dark face like a coconut.

The Power of Prayer and Availability

I look back at this incident and marvel at how much we demand of ourselves yet underestimate the power of prayer and availability. Unlike what people told me, God did not require me to have a specialty in pediatrics or a PhD to help. All He required of Cliff and me was our hearts yielded to prayer and the availability to be His hands and feet. When you have nothing but five loaves and two fish to feed more than five thousand people, that's precisely the moment not to give up but to present your little to God. With a willing heart, anyone can serve.

God doesn't want pretentious offerings. He's looking for broken, emptied vessels completely yielded to the power of prayer. The truth is, no matter how qualified we think we need to be, we'll find ourselves in situations beyond our capabilities. Only God's grace can provide answers to our greatest fears.

Through prayer, our little multiplies. Through prayer, miracles happen. After all, in Dembe's dream, it was the Man in white with a face so bright it could not be seen who stood behind me restoring Divine's precious life.

If you're weary, discouraged, and overwhelmed, will you set aside your insufficiencies and trust God with your little? Will you see beyond the present and wait on His future promises? You see, even though the training curricula and healthcare partnerships I'd worked so hard for seemed to die with Miremba, God reminded me that this one life saved through offering a prayer of faith sowed seeds of eternal significance. Even though I didn't receive the promise of systemic healthcare transformation, the vision that propelled me in my work, God provided something better: a testimony of faith that I believe will over the years encourage many more people to go into the unknown with their five loaves and two fish than to stay put where they are in comfort.

Likewise, if you see your vision and dreams slipping away, will you remind yourself that God, in His goodness, has something better in His future plans for you? It may not look like what we want or expect, but through faith and if we stay faithful, we will inherit His eternal rewards.

You might not lead a sprawling ministry or own a world-famous enterprise or be applauded as a groundbreaking pioneer. Yet God's scales are different. As we live our lives as witnesses of His faith, He provides us something better through His greater, eternal purposes we may not yet see. Your faithful sowing might blaze the trail for others behind you; your humble plowing might inspire generations beyond your own.

Today, Divine is a preteen. When I made those phone calls trying to save her life, I never imagined the woman she would be one day, the change maker she could one day become in her community. Yet God sees the future. All He requires of us is faithfulness in the present. While you may not receive the fullness of His promises now, know this: someday in eternity, you most certainly will. The equivalent of a little phone call you make in obedience to His will may one day grow into a young person who changes the world years after your death.

Don't give up. Don't give in. Give your little to God and let Him reveal the fullness of His promises in His timeline, His way. Dream brave.

FOR REFLECTION

1. How far from fulfilling your dreams do you think you are right now?
2. How does that make you feel?
3. What can you focus on in the present to enable you to stay faithful?

NEXT STEPS

1. List your greatest disappointments in your journey of pursuing your God-given dream.
2. Spend ten minutes visualizing the fullness of God's promises to you.

3. Write down commitments you'll continue to make on a daily basis to work toward this dream, even if it might not be fulfilled in your lifetime.

PRAYER

God, seeing how far away I am from the fruition of the dream you've given me can be so discouraging. At times I'm paralyzed with disappointment. Yet I know that all I do in obedience each day is sowing into a future promise that may be fulfilled beyond my lifetime. Grant me the grace to believe in and wait on your future promises each day. Help me stay committed and faithful to my daily tasks. Amen.

9

take risks by faith

> By faith they passed through the Red Sea as by dry land, whereas the Egyptians, attempting to do so, were drowned.
>
> —Hebrews 11:29

"ARE YOU OKAY?"

Cliff groaned as he staggered out of the bathroom, nearly falling over.

Illness could not have struck in a less timely fashion. We had just completed a ten-hour journey back from a village where we facilitated the graduation ceremony of a cohort of African Bible school students when Cliff began to retch.

"We're supposed to leave tomorrow morning for Rwanda to teach at their Bible school. How are we going to make it like this?" I asked him.

"I'll be fine after some rest. Don't worry."

But all that night, Cliff stayed up in the bathroom, a gastrointestinal mess.

"Oh, Lord," I muttered. "Please heal Cliff. He has to drive for two days for us to reach Rwanda." I didn't have a driving license to help.

We'd seen what African highways looked like—interminable strips of tarmac road weaving between rugged mountains and empty fields that stretched for miles without a sign of civilization in sight, restroom stops few and far between. I imagined my husband fainting at the wheel or teetering over a pit latrine while swatting away swarms of houseflies.

At breakfast, I looked at Cliff's face drained of blood. He couldn't eat a morsel. I bit my lower lip. What should we do? What if he deteriorated to the point of dehydration in the middle of nowhere?

"It's your call, sweetheart," I said.

I ate my breakfast quietly, slowly, seeing through Cliff's thoughts. Dozens of students from all over Rwanda were already making their way to the Bible school. Many had made sacrifices to be present, and finding replacements for us at such short notice would be impossible.

I looked down, my feet shifting. *Oh, Lord,* I prayed silently, *give me faith and peace to submit to whatever Cliff decides.*

Suddenly, Cliff looked up and said, "God's given me peace. We should go. If I'm going to be miserable sitting here anyway, I might as well be miserable driving over!"

This did not make sense. It could be dangerous. Yet I sensed God's quiet voice say, *You asked for faith to submit to Cliff's decision. Trust Me to help you cross the border.*

Hebrews 11:29 says, "By faith they passed through the Red Sea as by dry land, whereas the Egyptians, attempting to do so, were drowned." In this story, Moses and the Israelites, called by God to leave Egypt, possessed faith to cross the Red Sea to escape the Egyptians. In contrast, the Egyptians, overcome with rashness and presumption, rushed in to meet their destruction.

The word *attempting* finds its root word in the Greek Πειρα (peira), which means to "trial, experiment, put to the test."[1] What this really reminds us of is the importance of acting in faith, for the same action in a mimicry of faith can have totally opposite outcomes if not done with an attitude of assurance in God. What was *faith* in the Israelites was *presumption* in the Egyptians.[2] How can the Red Sea part? That defies any natural law! Yet activated by the faith of the Israelites, God intervened.

Have you been in a situation that required boldness to move through a difficult transition? These verses tell us how key it is for us to be guided by faith. Even after witnessing so many miracles, they constantly complained: "If only we had died in this wilderness! . . . Would it not be better for us to return to Egypt?" (Numbers 14:2–3). God had promised them freedom. Yet because of temporal difficulties and perceived risks, they wanted out, preferring to return to Egypt for the superficial comforts of life even though they would be slaves again.

Do we, too, feel tempted to return to where safety holds its beguiling enchantment over us? Like the Israelites, I'm sometimes tempted to turn back.

Our choice to follow God is a risk itself. By walking through our Red Sea, we risk the chance of being swallowed by its waves! What we must focus on, then, is the certainty of God's promise. Why? In Romans 8:18, Paul said, "I consider that the sufferings of this present time are not worthy to be compared with the glory which shall be revealed in us." This reminds us that we can't let the illusion of security rob us of the opportunity to witness the greatest miracle of all. Here, this amazing miracle reflected two victories—the Israelites' salvation from the Egyptians but also their baptism of faith into the covenant of God (1 Corinthians 10:2).[3] When we take risks by faith and pass the test, we are baptized into faith itself.

Next I'd like to share two personal stories that illustrate our need to be guided by faith, not sense. I hope they will encourage you to take the risks worth taking—without turning back.

Be Guided by Faith, Not Mere Sense

As I texted prayer supporters back home, a faithful prayer warrior replied, *Praying in faith that as you cross the border, Cliff will be healed in Jesus' name!*

I smiled wryly. With Cliff's immunocompromised condition, I knew this nasty bug could last for weeks. For him to be free of symptoms as we crossed the border would require nothing short of a miracle.

We left, and the road ahead seemed to stretch on forever. The sky, a canvas of pillowy clouds, kissed the earth over hilly horizons as our little car bobbed up and down undulating roads.

"A bottle of orange Fanta, a roll of toilet paper, and God is all I need," hummed Cliff weakly as he drove. I looked at him in disbelief.

In the early evening, we arrived at Lake Bunyonyi, its name meaning "lake of many birds," for an overnight stopover. Cliff rushed to the bathroom. I looked over the lake from a thatched mud hut, a heavy foreboding brewing cold under the low, bruised clouds.

I remembered my friend's prayer. For Cliff to fully recover as we crossed the border into Rwanda seemed impossible. But desperate, I held on to Matthew 21:21. Jesus' disciples had asked Him why a fig tree He'd declared would never again bear fruit had withered so quickly, and He said, "If you have faith and do not doubt, you will not only do what was done to the fig tree, but also if you say to this mountain, 'Be removed and be cast into the sea,' it will be done."

Then rains poured down in blinding sheets. Sky and lake merged into one gray slate. And as Cliff continued to purge (I'll spare you the details), I sent an email to my infectious disease professor, begging for advice. "She probably won't even see this in time," I said aloud.

But my phone immediately pinged! *Discontinue Flagyl,* she replied. *Give a stat dose of 1000mg azithromycin, plus some Imodium. Given his medical history, he needs more rest and might even need intravenous hydration.*

Wild jungle, red-dirt roads, and mud-hut villages stretched for acres around us. Where would I get any of that?

We hardly slept as Cliff remained so ill and the rains, relentless, beat against the thatched roof. Hours later, the sun yawned awake. Clouds hung low, heavy and hollow. We set off, our eyes sunken. I stared out the window as rolling hills gave way to rows of concrete shacks where people sold drinks, snacks, and knickknacks.

Then I jerked out of my seat. A pharmacy! My heart leaped, then sank like a stone in quicksand. A mere hole in the wall, its hand-painted signboard crumbled and hanging sideways, this place looked questionable—more like an over-the-counter first aid station. If we got lucky, they might have a few basic antibiotics, but surely not azithromycin. And even if they did, they would surely need a prescription, which we didn't have.

My frenzied thoughts whittled my hopes down to a grain of sand, but I told Cliff to stop the car. "I must give it a shot."

Inside, a little bespectacled Indian man busied himself behind a plastic screen, scribbling on notebooks.

"Do you have azithromycin?" I asked.

He pursed his lips. Disappointed at this apparent no, I turned to leave. But then he pushed a tiny metal foil, folded into crisp quarters, under the screen.

"What's this?" I asked.

Without looking up, he muttered, "You asked for it. Azithromycin. That's two thousand five hundred shillings."

A dollar? It cost a dollar!

I sprinted back to the car, tears in my eyes. "I found it, Cliff! It's a miracle! I got it!"

Cliff immediately washed the medicine down with Fanta.

As we crossed to Rwanda an hour later, drab concrete melted into a wash of green. Cool, crisp winds kissed our faces. A wild flock of Ugandan crested cranes flew regally over us, so close I thought I could touch them. The presence of a misty dreamscape was breathtaking.

Then Cliff said to me, "I feel a bit peckish. Got a banana? Make that two!" This was the first time he'd been interested in food for days!

As I remembered my friend's prayer, goose bumps washed all over me. Every natural law and logic pointed to danger and ill health. There was no way we could have crossed our Red Sea. Yet as we stepped out in faith into the unknown, God met us. He pushed back the waters and made a way—an impossible way!

As the Israelites stood in front of the Red Sea, fear gripped them (Exodus 14:10–12), and I'm certain they were tempted to turn back. Yet Pharaoh's armies at their heels made that impossible, forcing them to exercise faith. In the same way, if Cliff and I had turned back midway, if we had not taken a further risk by faith, we'd never have found that pharmacy or experienced our "Red Sea moment" with God!

Understand the Illusion of Security

Do you sometimes ponder how thin the line is between courageous, faith-filled risk-taking and foolhardy gambling? I do. Yet this brings to mind how, perhaps more often than we'd like, God requires us to step out of our comfort zone to get His work done. Research suggests we make as many as thirty-five thousand decisions a day.[4] Every day we weigh risks for our benefit. The problem with this, John Piper says, is that we underestimate our ignorance. We are not God. While human wisdom is valuable, it falls far short of God's (1 Corinthians 3:19).[5]

The choice to stay home instead of leaving to follow the Lord's call might sound logical, but our house could catch fire. The choice to keep our jobs instead of obeying His call to start a new venture might make financial sense, but companies can go bust. We forget security is an illusion, a mirage we make up. John Piper also says, "The tragic hypocrisy is that the enchantment of security lets us take risks every day for ourselves but paralyzes us from taking risks for others on the Calvary road of love. We are deluded and think that it may jeopardize a security that in fact does not even exist."[6]

What kinds of false illusions of security have you made up for yourself? It could be a world painted with ideals of a stable job, a rising career, a beautiful home, or getting your children into the best schools. What kinds of decisions have you made to feed that world without realizing they were "risks" to you and your family? After all, it's not every day that we consider saying yes to a lucrative job offer or signing our children up for summer camp and enrichment classes as real "risks."

Yet through a different lens, they very well could be. For what greater risk is there than to expose yourself to the allures of riches and status? What greater danger is there than to expose your children to the notion that academic success is the central tenet from which we gain our significance? These are all real temptations to idolatry and threats to our inheriting eternal life. The truth is these are the risks we willingly take every day without considering their "unexpected outcomes." Yet when it comes to God's call for us to step out, many of us immediately classify those risks as frighteningly dangerous.

Like Moses and the Israelites, we must let our faith take us higher. In the natural, entering the Red Sea would mean a hundred percent chance of drowning. At least while battling the Egyptians on dry land, there might be a small chance of victory. Yet they believed, and their faith activated God's intervention. You see, the mirage of security lets us take risks every day for ourselves but immobilizes us from taking risks for God. Our faith in risk-taking for God through obedience and wisdom, however, is exactly what activates the miraculous. Don't you want to be a part of that adventure?

Back to our trip to Rwanda, God's lesson for us was not over. On the way back, I thought we would die.

It all happened so fast. Blinding lights, a sharp swerve, the sound of crushing metal, and an explosive smattering of glass into shards. I sat frozen in the passenger seat, my heart thumping in my ears.

A truck surging at us with brazen chutzpah had rounded a blind bend and pushed us precariously close to the cliff's edge. Had force, friction, and velocity played a different roulette, we would have been killed. I envisioned our car flicked into the bottomless valley below like a tiny cake crumb off a table, our ribs cracking as our bodies smashed against branches thick as pillars before being crunched dead by gravity and metal.

Thick, dense rain forest reached high into the sky, blocking out sunlight here at the aptly named "Bwindi mountain," the word *bwindi* meaning "impenetrable." The leaves of trees coalesced into one thick blanket above us. Dark and misty, this painted the perfect backdrop for a calamitous end—with no cell phone reception or even telephones for miles, nor anyone else in sight.

An angry voice snapped me out of my stupor.

"*Banange* [Oh my gosh!]!" snarled the truck driver, drawing out each syllable in his native language. His hot, burly voice pummeled at us. "You should drive on left!"

The serpentine dirt roads, thread-thin, snaked around the mountains. How could right or left be discerned? Only caution and chance gave one escape.

In Rwanda, everyone had told us, "You *must* visit the endangered silverback gorillas on your way back. It's a once-in-a-lifetime experience. Support local tourism!"

Attracted by the allure of adventure, we signed up confidently. After all, what could go wrong? The website boasted an unforgettable experience. But we didn't know how wild the journey there would be, how fiercely feral and rough the terrain was. We didn't expect a near-death experience.

I often think back on these two experiences—Cliff's being so ill and our road accident—grateful for the lessons drawn from them. They remind me of what poor judges of risk we are. Who would have thought that some wanderlust sightseeing would bring us so close to death, far closer than when driving on unknown roads with severe illness? But I understand now. Presumption plus adventure can often lead to destruction. No matter how logical things may seem, being led by what appears to make sense over faith can go wrong.

Remember the Egyptians. It would make sense that they should survive crossing the Red Sea since the Israelites who just went ahead had! But no, it is faith that carries us through risky endeavors. In case you're overwhelmed by how dangerous it is to cross the Red Sea, walk the road of Calvary, and put all you are on the line to fulfill the dreams God has for your life, remember the thousands of decisions we make every day put us closer to the cliff's edge than the occasional clarion call to obedience by God.

My hope is that as you recognize those risks, you might change your perception of risk-taking, recalibrate risk-taking, so you might, by faith, wisely take the risks God presents to you in your journey of pursuing the dreams He has for your life—risks worth taking no matter the cost.

FOR REFLECTION

1. What risks does pursuing God's call for your life pose to you?
2. What allures of comfort and security hold you back?
3. What is at stake if you turn back?

NEXT STEPS

1. In a chart like this one, list risks you face in your journey of obedience. An example would be the risk of losing your house, another risk that concerned me.

Risks I face in my journey of obedience:	**Verses that anchor my faith in God:**
Losing my home	"The LORD has been my defense, and my God the rock of my refuge" (Psalm 94:22)

2. For every risk, list a Bible verse that anchors your faith in God in the second column.
3. Remind yourself of what's at stake if you do not pursue your dream, then write that down.

PRAYER

God, my transition to "cross over the Red Sea" feels risky. I fear drowning, and at times I want to turn back. Help me rely on faith, not sense, and to pursue boldness, not mere adventure. Give me your assurance that my faith activates your anointing. Help me take bold risks by faith. Help me to dream brave. How I long to see your miracles! Amen.

10

fix your eyes on greater riches

> By faith Moses, when he became of age, refused to be called the son of Pharaoh's daughter, choosing rather to suffer affliction with the people of God than to enjoy the passing pleasures of sin, esteeming the reproach of Christ greater riches than the treasures in Egypt; for he looked to the reward.
>
> —Hebrews 11:24–26

HYSTERICAL, BLOODCURDLING shrieks pierced the air, and the hair on my arms stood on end as Cliff and I exchanged knowing looks of dread. The person who'd been groaning at the clinic next door for so long, who we thought to be an elderly man, had no doubt finally died. As a cacophony of unrestrained screams continued to erupt in a maelstrom of grief, I imagined the drama unfolding—a wife unraveling, pounding the floor; a brother, no doubt with hands clenched into fists, beating his chest; children and distant relatives, weeping, inconsolable.

We fled to a quiet spot at the foot of the hill, where I prayed aloud, "Why has it been so hard to serve here, Lord?"

As I shared previously, we hadn't slept through the night for months. Disco music from a nearby bar shack pounded well past midnight. In the monsoon season, squalls of driving rain seeped through the broken louvers and soaked our floor-laid mattress. On other days, choking smoke from burning garbage enshrouded our home while a nearby bonfire crackled.

Earlier that week, Cliff and I had tossed and turned to the ebb and flow of those loud groans from the clinic next door. Anxiety had sliced into me as strangers from far-flung villages lingered near our front door, waiting. I felt unnerved watching them, feeling watched. We spoke in whispers, not knowing who might hear. The air grew tense with foreboding.

It didn't help that Cliff and I had been struggling with recurrent nightmares. He, of zombies, bloodthirsty wolves, and petite-sized impish spirits dancing within our home. Me, of spirits threatening to strangle me, leaving me in a cold sweat. The nightmares and ominous groans both cast a ghostly, macabre shadow on us. (Later, we discovered that our clinic-turned-living-quarters was once a pediatric ward for children dying of HIV.)

"Why, God, did we have to come all the way here?" I continued to pray. "Do you know how much I gave up? These days, everyone is doing missions digitally. Surely with better sleep back home, we could do more to help those in need, even if virtually!"

Cliff wrapped his arm, thick and strong, around me as I sobbed into his chest.

"Let me read you 2 Corinthians 4:17–18," he said, opening the Bible he'd brought along. "'For our light affliction, which is but for a moment, is working for us a far more exceeding and eternal weight of glory, while we do not look at the things which are seen, but at the things which are not seen. For the things which are seen are temporary, but the things which are not seen are eternal.'"

Deep down, I knew God had called us to serve in Uganda, that this was part of His and my dream for me to serve as a medical missionary to the poor. And even though I struggled with missing city comforts, my peace and quiet, and little luxuries, I knew this form of incarnational living, with all its hardships, reflected

Christ's life. He had the chance to rule and reign from the heavenlies as God's Son, yet He humbled Himself to love us in human form, even enduring death on a cross (Philippians 2:8).

Hebrews 11:24–26 says, "By faith Moses, when he became of age, refused to be called the son of Pharaoh's daughter, choosing rather to suffer affliction with the people of God than to enjoy the passing pleasures of sin, esteeming the reproach of Christ greater riches than the treasures in Egypt; for he looked to the reward."

What could have made Moses prefer adoption by an unseen King over the Pharaoh's daughter? It could be nothing but faith in what God had in store for his life to help his people.[1] Continuing to live as this woman's adopted son, Moses could have had ongoing prestige, wealth, and honor. Yet at the age of forty, he gave up his aristocratic lifestyle, choosing instead to "suffer affliction with the people of God."[2] Moses, like Jesus, intentionally decided to relinquish his comfort and be with God's people, treasuring his obedience to God as of greater value than anything the palace had to offer.

The Greek root word for "reproach" is ὀνειδισμὸν (oneidismon), which means "disgrace."[3] But why would anyone consider the disgrace of Christ as greater riches? Why—and how—did Moses consider Christ's disgrace and shame of greater value than all of Egypt's riches? What a puzzling calculation!

But the phrase *for he looked to the reward* gives us a clue, for its root word in the Greek, ἀποβλέπω (apoblepó), means "to look away from all else at an object."[4] Moses, seeing by faith the invisible, was enraptured by the eternal inheritance he had in Christ and counted "all things loss for the excellence of the knowledge of Christ" (Philippians 3:8). In that moment he understood what Jesus said in Mark 8:36: "For what will it profit a man if he gains the whole world, and loses his own soul?" And eternal rewards he did get: friendship and a legacy of faith with God.

Faith reshuffles our value system. Through God's lens, we calculate differently. With Him, we receive faith, joy, and the audacity to give up all we own when asked in order to attain the one treasure we desire most—Christ Himself (Matthew 13:44–46).

In our world today, many will try to convince you that you can always help others *and* stay comfortable. You can serve the poor *and* enjoy the best the world can offer. After all, with surging technological advances, serving can easily take digital forms. Nonetheless, at specific times in our journeys of faith, God may call us to give up our comforts to "suffer affliction with the people of God" (Hebrews 11:25). When He calls you, will you be ready?

Let me tell you the rest of my story, what happened after we heard those bloodcurdling screams in Uganda. This became a vulnerable story of humiliation, gleaned from the hardships of living with the poor, without the comfort we sometimes yearned for. Ultimately, I hope it will challenge you to leave your comfort zone to suffer with those who suffer when God calls you to do so. To ultimately fix your eyes on Christ's greater riches and savor His greater reward.

Look to an Eternal Reward

Now dozens of people had arrived. A civil servant in his white-collared shirt, sweat stains spreading under his armpits, texted busily on his smartphone. Elderly matrons, large as barrels, glided as though footless in their flowy Ugandan *gomez* dresses, muttering in prayerful intercession. Teenagers in hand-me-down Linkin' Park shirts, young mothers with breasts ready to feed their babies, and tall men with coarse hands all found a spot in our front yard.

As they all peered curiously into our home, we became zoo animals in our own cage. Passersby pointed at us constantly, saying, "*Mzungu* [foreigner]."

Suddenly, a wave of emotions flooded my chest. For months, I'd felt watched. I'd walk down to the store at the foot of the hill with people asking me, "Is your hair for sale? Can I feel it?" Others shouted, "You from China? Korea? Japan?" Young boys whooped and whistled, then shouted, "Jackie Chan! Hoo-hah! Hoo-hah!" I felt ashamed for wanting some privacy yet bristled with frustration. Sharp angles stuck out of me, needing to be sanded down.

Once, alone and exhausted from this unwanted spotlight, I wailed. How I wished for the luxury of buying a bar of soap without being drawn into curious conversation! But though grudgingly, I tried to accept these inconveniences as part and parcel of serving the Lord.

Now I reminded myself to be grateful, but my heart, blighted by bitterness, festered with resentment. Cliff and I spoke in whispers, carrying an uncertain foreboding. We tried to ignore the peering crowd, tried to close the windows, but people looked on curiously. The air in our little home felt like cracked glass. I paced, restless, longing for distraction.

I confess, I held little sympathy for these dozens of uninvited "guests." Those polyphonic Afro beats that boomed through the night had worn us down, and all I wanted was peace and quiet! A chilling self-entitlement lanced through me. *How long will they stay? When can we have our privacy back?* My thoughts swam in my head, and I was groggy with self-pity. *Why did I come to Uganda? Wouldn't it have been enough to serve God as a doctor in my home country?*

When we returned home, part of the grieving assemblage had spilled onto our front porch, into our chairs, blocking our entrance. Suddenly, something in me, something that had tried its best to withstand, to withhold, to endure without breaking throughout the previous months, bent backward just a little more. Then it snapped in two, and a rash eagerness to lash out overcame me.

My words of anger went straight for a large woman in a yellow wrapper with jiggly arms who wore an air of harmlessness, and I measured every word, before announcing, "Those are *our* chairs, and this is a private residence."

I braced myself, waiting for a response of remorse. Instead, the elderly matriarch stood, her thin lips turned downward. "Do you *share* chairs in your country?" she asked. "This is Uganda. And in Uganda, we share chairs."

My heart raced. Blood throbbed into my ears. How cocky and self-entitled she was! I shut our door quickly behind me.

As if to prove a point, the matriarch gathered even more family members to sit outside our home, to carry on their family conference. I watched them from inside, nursing my humiliation. *After all I've given up, how can they treat me like this?*

Then I sensed God telling me that all this while I'd let my self-righteousness and superiority grow. Whenever I felt slighted, I insulated myself in self-pity, nursing my hurts. Tears ran down my face. But the Lord, filled with tenderness, whispered to me, *What do you count as your rights?*

Hebrews 11:24–26 became alive to me. At the age of twenty-six, I had left my career, home, and riches in Singapore to live among the poor in Uganda. Like Moses, I chose to give up my rights to a life of comfort to suffer with God's people. Yet in contrast to Moses, who esteemed "the reproach of Christ greater riches than the treasures in Egypt," I grumbled. I longed to return to my homeland. In moments of hardship, I murmured easily about water issues and power cuts and pounding disco music at night.

I felt the Lord smiling gently at me, saying, *Are you fixing your eyes on My reward?*

"But I've sacrificed so much for you, Lord!" I cried out, surprising myself.

You're looking to the past. Can you look forward to My eternal reward?

At once, I understood Moses' seemingly ridiculous choice to choose the worst of a Christ-following life over a life of luxury. He did so because he looked ahead to the reward. He could do so because he was propelled by faith. You see, faith looks to the future. It transforms our present thinking and propels us toward God's destiny for our lives. All this while, I had looked to the past—griping about the house, career path, and academic pursuits I'd left behind.

But God nudged my vision upward and forward. *Following Me is about looking to what is ahead. Fix your eyes on My greater rewards.*

When I caught sight of God's eternal rewards for obeying Him, I gasped in revelation. How pitiable my sacrifices looked compared to what Christ sacrificed for me—His very life!

Later that afternoon, a health center nurse walked past me.

"So the elderly man passed on, yeah?" I said. "What hard news."

The nurse shook her head, tsk-tsking away. "Oh, it wasn't the grandpa who died. It was a young toddler. So unexpected. The doctors tried so hard."

Immediately, my eyes were opened, and I let out a desperate cry of relief, a confessional cry of horror that I might have let myself go crazy in fighting for those chairs of mine.

Our values of right and wrong, which might be so easily circumscribed in our own cultures, can often be unceremoniously overturned in another. I thought borrowing without asking was clearly incorrect, but in an intensely relational, communal culture, to assume that was wrong.

Self-entitlement loses its compass when we realize it has nothing to anchor itself.

To Serve, Not to Be Served

When Jesus came for His earthly ministry, He came to serve, not to be served. The word *incarnation* is what theologians use to describe how Jesus took on flesh to be with us.[5] Though He, the Son of God, possessed every right to exercise His heavenly rights, He succumbed Himself to spit, shame, and dishonor simply to obey His Father's call.

For all I thought I'd sacrificed to serve these locals, the truth revealed itself: I had more to learn from them than they had to learn from me. By choosing, in faith, to suffer affliction with God's people, I learned to esteem the hardships, the disgrace, and the reproaches for the heavenly rewards of gaining character—that of patience, self-denial, and faithfulness.

There in Africa that day, I discovered the humility of sharing chairs. And I gleaned invaluably greater rewards—eternal treasures of compassion, empathy, and love from suffering affliction with the people of God.

In your journey to pursue God's call for your life—in pursuing His dreams for you—do you ever wish you could be more comfortable? In a digital age, do you prefer to retreat behind screens? Many of us long for the heroic legacy of Moses' life. Yet we forget the years he spent in the wilderness suffering the Israelites' complaints daily without the comforts of the palace. In John 15:12, Jesus encourages us, "Love each other as I have loved you" (NIV). Loving others through our physical presence and incarnational living cannot be more biblical.

If you're struggling with the lackluster humdrum of your daily life to be physically present for those you love, know that Jesus came as a baby, then lay in a makeshift cradle in the dirt and embraced thirty years of ordinary living before His three years of ministry began. If you're wrestling with leaving your comfort zone to suffer hardships along with His people, know that He endured spit and scorn to love His children. But He could do that because He fixed His eyes on greater riches and His eternal reward.

Like Moses, can we open our hearts to treasuring Christ above all? Can we be so enraptured by His invisible, eternal rewards of the future that we count the momentary afflictions of incarnational living as loss? Will we be willing to leave our lives of comfort to enter into His divine call for our lives?

If so, we might be surprised to find ourselves delighting in staying faithful to the challenges of God's call for our lives: loving the unlovely, grieving with the sick, visiting the lonely, and living among the poor, if not as Cliff and I did in Uganda but in some way of His choosing. Only then will we come to cherish the extraordinary ways God uses our moments of pain, of hardship, to develop in us eternal fruit of the Holy Spirit, treasures of far greater value in eternity than any riches here on earth.

FOR REFLECTION

1. What did you or do you have to give up in order to follow God's call for your life? What "passing pleasures of sin" did you or do you have to surrender?
2. What "greater treasures" have you gleaned from suffering difficult situations?
3. How has "esteeming the reproach of Christ" and looking to His reward changed your perspective and choices?

NEXT STEPS

1. If you're enduring a particularly difficult affliction, take it to the Lord and ask Him for grace and mercy.
2. Write down one fruit of the Spirit God is developing in your current circumstance that will be among your eternal riches.
3. Schedule time to ask the Lord to give you a vision of what greater rewards and eternal pleasures He has for you. As He reveals the vision to you, write it down or draw it.

PRAYER

God, today I intentionally choose to refuse the allures of our world. Instead, I choose to fix my eyes on greater riches and look ahead to your heavenly rewards. Grant me the kind of faith that transforms my present thoughts and propels me toward your destiny. Let the glory of your future rewards give me strength to serve the broken and unlovely even when it requires endurance. Help me to see beyond the hardships of my present so I may look to a future of eternal riches with you. Help me to keep dreaming brave. Amen.

11

sojourn with God in faith

> These all died in faith, not having received the promises, but having seen them afar off were assured of them, embraced them and confessed that they were strangers and pilgrims on the earth. For those who say such things declare plainly that they seek a homeland.
>
> —Hebrews 11:13–14

THE QUESTIONS SEEMED NEVER-ENDING.

"Where will you stay when you get back to Singapore?"

"Will you reapply for surgical training?"

"Your savings must be all wiped out by now. What are your financial plans for the future?"

Our year in Uganda had passed, and as the time drew near for us to return to Singapore, questions from friends and family flooded in. My yearlong period of no-pay leave had come to an end, and I had to return home to complete the remaining years of my compulsory five-year bond with the Singapore government as a doctor. But I had no answers to the torrent of questions.

As I prepared for the journey home, I browsed the lives of my peers on social media. I could see a new luxury to their rhythms, now engraved in comfort—passports sagging with the weight of visa stamps to conferences around the world, photos of exquisite plates in fine-dining restaurants, professionally airbrushed profile photos I didn't have.

Despite the lessons I'd learned over the past months, their glossy lives captivated me, and a part of me ached while another part felt stained with shame. I sighed with disappointment at my ego, hungry to be polished by shimmery things. I feared that underneath my seemingly pious life, people would see the flashes of regret I had for things I longed for in the present and future. A small resentment grew in my knowing that things like housing, holidays, and little luxuries slid into the spaces of other people's lives so easily compared to mine.

And then I resented the shallowness of my character beginning to emerge. I would remind myself of all the right Bible verses, like when Jesus said it would be "easier for a camel to go through the eye of a needle than for a rich man to enter the kingdom of God" (Mark 10:25). And that following God was the right thing to do. But deep inside, a war I didn't understand broke out. I simply wanted the comforts of a place I could call my permanent home. But after we returned to Singapore, how soon would God lead us to yet another temporary home?

A part of me didn't want to return to Singapore. For days, I daydreamed about cutting off ties and disappearing into rural villages in Africa, abandoning my remaining bond with the government. We had begun to adapt to Uganda. Projects were gaining traction. Accommodation in Singapore was difficult to find, housing prices had skyrocketed, and since Cliff's workplace and mine were at opposite ends of the country, the fairest housing location would be central, the most expensive part of Singapore. I shuddered knowing that a small studio apartment in a run-down neighborhood in the city rented for over two thousand dollars a month.

Even though we were still in Uganda, our time there had taken on a sepia tone, as if it belonged to a world far away.

In an idle moment of curiosity, I counted the number of train stations between Cliff's workplace and mine, finding the midpoint in a quiet neighborhood called Marymount. I hoped we could find a decent rental there. So I scoured all possible online sources. But I found none. Public housing in the area was scarce. Most properties were private—large terrace houses, expansive bungalows, towering built-to-fit mansions for the upper class.

One night I bared my heart to God. *Isn't it unfair that Cliff and I have to keep moving? This is uneconomical—financially and time-wise. Why can't we just stay put here?*

Then Hebrews 11:13–14 came to mind: "These all died in faith, not having received the promises, but having seen them afar off were assured of them, embraced them and confessed that they were strangers and pilgrims on the earth. For those who say such things declare plainly that they seek a homeland."

God reminded me that though Abraham, Sarah, Isaac, and Jacob sojourned from place to place without ever experiencing the full promise of seeing their descendants fill the earth, Abraham's faith to fully believe in God's power to make him the father of many nations was "accounted to him for righteousness" (Romans 4:22). As temporary residents on earth, Abraham and his offspring traveled like pilgrims both literally and figuratively. Even though their desire to seek a homeland was real, they embraced being foreigners leading nomadic lives, bravely following God to where He called them because of their assurance that God knew what He was doing, that He had a permanent heavenly dwelling place for them.

I felt God challenge me. Could I, too, trust that He had prepared a glorious heavenly home for me (John 14:2)? Was my faith in that vision enough for me to hold on to and suffer the inconveniences of a nomadic life on earth? Tears streamed down my cheeks. While part of me understood that my "citizenship is in heaven" (Philippians 3:20), other parts of me still desperately ached for a comfortable home of ease, stability, and convenience.

In my tussle with the Lord, I felt Him loosen my grip on our home in Uganda, asking me to come to Him with open palms so He could lead us to our next temporary home. Even though I didn't want to leave, God reminded me of the value of honoring my word and returning home to finish my bond. I sensed Him say, *As you honor Me, so will I honor you.* As He spoke those words, I felt a shift in my spirit.

God Sojourns with Us

Perhaps you, like Abraham, have yet to see God's promises and dreams for you come to pass. Perhaps you've been worn out by the inconveniences of pursuing His call through shifting seasons. After all, most of us aspire to things like owning a home and increasing our financial security.

I'd like to share a story I hope will encourage you to embrace your identity as one of "strangers and pilgrims on the earth" (Hebrews 11:13), as you sojourn bravely toward heaven. I hope it will encourage you to hold lightly on to your earthly homes and possessions and to give yourself wholly to God. For those who put their faith in Him, life on earth is a mere transit stop to an everlasting home.

One evening I received a text message from a medical school mentor with photos of a house in Singapore and its address. The cryptic message read, *Do you want to stay here?*

I let out a long sigh. Clearly, my mentor didn't understand our financial situation. The photos showed several massive rooms in a colossal bungalow. Also clearly, the rental price was beyond our means. Otherwise, I speculated, we'd be sharing the home with other renters, which we didn't want to do. After all our housing challenges in Africa, we desperately craved privacy.

I glanced at the Westlake address and breathed a sigh of relief. It sounded too far from the city center. I had just typed in return

No, thank you when Cliff, peering over my shoulder, stopped me from sending it.

"You never know," he said casually, typing the address into his own phone.

"Never know what?" I was a little irritated.

"Wai Jia." Cliff's tone became more serious. "Westlake is in Marymount. It's right next to Marymount train station. Isn't that what you've been praying for?"

I was too afraid to be hopeful.

How much is the rent? I texted. *Will we stay with other people?*

I had many more questions, but I assumed the answers to these two would swiftly close out this option.

The reply read, *Answer me first, Wai Jia—is this a good location for you?*

Pressure built behind my eyes. *Yes,* I texted back. *The location is uncanny, because it's at the midpoint of both our new workplaces. I'm unfamiliar with that neighborhood, but it's exactly where we prayed to find something.*

My eyes widened when I read the next text.

So . . . a gentleman who has been reading about the work you and Cliff do owns an empty two-story bungalow he's hoping to sell, but he hasn't been able to. He's asking if you can house-sit for him for a year or so for free. He just asks if you could pay his gardener $80 a month to maintain his yard. Would that be okay?

"Would that be okay?" I laughed through tears of gratitude and replied, *I am speechless.*

Yet in the nights after, I tottered under many anxieties. Would the house be quiet? Would it be peaceful there? Would the neighbors be nice? Were there any pest issues? How could this be so easy?

As we bade goodbye to our home atop a hill on our last evening in Africa, from our front porch I watched the monkeys cross the barbed wire on the fence nearby one last time. Nostalgically, I told Cliff, "I will miss this sight very much."

God Is Our Secure Refuge

After arriving in Singapore, we stood in the bungalow feeling small. Why? Because it was mammoth-sized—a mansion, really. The high ceilings made it seem twice as big as it already was. A single room was almost as large as the entire living space we had in Uganda. It was old, and there was a tiny leak at the corner of the house, but even the kitchen and yard were huge.

The neighbors spilled onto the road as soon as we moved in, welcoming us, waving, dropping off desserts. At night, the air rang loud only with the sound of crickets. The cool wind from the nature reserve nearby blew in. Within a mere week, strangers and friends alike gifted us all kinds of secondhand and brand-new furniture to furnish our new home.

One afternoon Cliff and I held hands in the side yard, in awe of the beautiful home we were suddenly stewarding. "Thank you, Lord," we whispered. Then suddenly, in the midst of the urban jungle that is Singapore, monkeys appeared out of nowhere, crossing our fence the way they had near our front porch in Uganda.

I squealed, "Cliff! God knows. He hears us!"

I marveled that God had not only answered my litany of prayer requests but thoughtfully blessed me with the sight of monkeys, the sight I'd wistfully thought I was bidding goodbye to forever as we left Uganda. A warm flush rose into my cheeks as I felt the Lord smiling down at me, saying, *I remember.*

The home was exactly what we needed, a sanctuary of rest to recover from the challenging year we'd had in Uganda. But six months into our stay, I received dreadful news: a member of parliament was scheduled to visit our home as a potential buyer. The thought of being ousted from this beautiful home prematurely and needing to find another shelter yet again nauseated me.

I resented this pilgrim's life. This house was precious, and the mere thought of the viewing request brought a sense of treasure already lost. Surely the property would be bought, but I hoped against all hope that it wouldn't.

I couldn't bear to be there the day the potential buyer visited. I imagined him rich, prosperous, eyeing the house and ogling its beauty. I cleaned and tidied with aching nostalgia, saddened to say goodbye to this home.

After he and his entourage left, I returned to a home littered with cookie crumbs, strewn from the living room up the stairs to the master bedroom like a cookie trail from the Brothers Grimm "Hansel and Gretel" fairy tale. In a self-righteous fit of anger, I complained to the housing agent in a text about this trespass, holding on to the house as if it were my very own.

Days passed without any word. Unable to contain my nervousness, I texted the landlord to ask how the viewing went. He replied that the potential buyer had turned down the property because the price was too high.

For the first time I dared ask how much the house was going for.

Eight and a half million.

I felt giddy, then suddenly I wanted to cry. Such was the generosity of God, our Father, that He would bless us with this place of refuge. We'd prayed for at least a single room flat in a public housing estate. But out of His extravagant love for us, He'd provided a beautiful home, one well beyond our expectations.

I learned an important lesson that day. Our prioritizing God's ways first compels Him to lavish His unspeakable love and extravagant provisions on us. As pilgrims, we have no choice but to trust Him for our daily manna, our next shelter. But when we do, He will not let us down. Both Cliff and I had resisted moving from place to place, not realizing God had something better in store for us. We had resented being pilgrims, not realizing He'd prepared a mansion for us in a future we had not yet seen.

At once, I felt an impartation of Abraham's faith deposited in me as I embraced the discomforts that come with pursuing the dreams He has for us, by looking toward a heavenly dwelling He has prepared for us. Though we were poor as sojourners, we were rich as heaven's citizens. Though we felt like weary wanderers, we were crowned by Christ in heaven. In emptying ourselves, God gave us more. In putting Him first, He made sure we knew we were foremost on His heart too. (He even remembered my monkeys!)

God showed me He had far more to offer, far more to give us than I could ever give up for Him.

A Deeper Surrender

To pursue the dreams God has called us to, we often need to surrender something. We may have to give up steady paychecks and lives of ease, stability, and comfort. Yet when we, like Abraham, see God's promises from far off and imagine how our dreams could impact future generations, we can find strength in the temporary discomforts of our sojourning. If we desire to honor Him with our hearts, to obey and move on with Him as He calls us into each and every season, He will provide the "manna and quail" we need at each step of the way. Like the actual manna (Exodus 16:31) and quail (16:13) He provided for the Israelites.

I think about how much I would have missed had I responded in rebellion and justified my staying in Uganda for my own self-righteous reasons. When we choose God's ways, even when they seem harder, He makes up fresh, creative ways to bless us. For He owns the universe and all that is within it. Is there anything too hard for Him?

As we house-sat, we enjoyed Singapore more and more. And when God called us to leave our home for Canada and the United States, this time to pursue my further studies at Johns Hopkins, we entertained the thought of staying put in the mansion instead.

Thankfully, God's still, small whisper nudged us: *Do you want to press on in your pilgrim's journey or stagnate in your spiritual walk?*

Cliff and I prayed and said, "Yes, Lord, we choose to press on with you."

On the day we left, the room we slept in became unbearably warm. At the peak of the hot season, the air-conditioning units had suddenly stopped working as if they'd decided, in unison, to let us know that God's provisions in this chapter of our lives had ended and fresh ones awaited elsewhere.

Friends, may you always be compelled by faith to move forward and onward with Christ. May we always allow the vision of His heavenly home for us to encourage us through our sojourns as we follow His dreams in our hearts. No matter how weary we may be in our earthly transitions, our final destination, sure as ever, awaits.

FOR REFLECTION

1. Recall a time you had to give up your rights or comforts in order to pursue God's dreams for your life. How did that feel?
2. What were some challenges you faced in terms of comparing your journey with that of others? How did you cope?
3. How does the assurance of a better, heavenly homeland change your perception of hardship on your pilgrimage?

NEXT STEPS

1. Which of God's promises to you have you yet seen come to pass? Remind yourself of when He's been faithful, then write those times down.
2. In the liminal space of waiting for the fruition of your dreams, what emotions and thoughts have you

experienced? Write them down. Then as you would with a friend, share them with God.

3. How does knowing that the patriarchs of faith mentioned in Hebrews 11 died without receiving God's promises impact the posture of your waiting? Write down one word the Lord reveals to you as you seek Him in prayer.

PRAYER

God, you know the hardships of sojourning. Jesus Himself left the comforts of heaven to sojourn on earth. Yet my soul is parched with weariness. I yearn for a sense of stability and belonging. Will you refresh my vision of your heavenly dwelling and promises for my life to help me sojourn bravely in faith on my pilgrimage? When I'm discouraged, revive me with the fullness of the fruition of all the dreams you have for my life, even if the fruits of it may be borne only in the generations to come. Amen.

12

surrender each step to God

> By faith Abraham obeyed when he was called to go out to the place which he would receive as an inheritance. And he went out, not knowing where he was going.
>
> —Hebrews 11:8

I HAVE SOMETHING TO TELL YOU. I've been offered a job here in Singapore, overseeing the entire missions department at our church."

When Cliff broke this news to me over dinner, a stiff silence followed. A sense of finality hung in the air, heavy and hollow. I wanted to be happy for him, but what felt like gravel lodged in my throat.

For months, we'd spent the evenings planning the future together. With hands clasped, fingers intertwined like lovers, we exchanged dreams. With Cliff, I could always be honest.

Months earlier, I'd shared how my dream of pursuing a Master of Public Health at Johns Hopkins in America had not faded. Instead, it had grown into something that heaved and wrestled within me. Even after first laying it down to obey God's call to marry Cliff, and then failing to submit my application a second time when He called us to Uganda, the dream continued to grow within me.

My mind brought me back to a time at an HIV clinic in Uganda, to an experience I mentioned in part in a previous chapter. I was trying to learn about the local conditions, and the psychiatrist at the clinic—a large, senior African man with a broad face and coarse hands—welcomed me to join him as he saw patients. I was grateful even though he hadn't looked at me when he said it.

When the first patient left the room, he asked me, "Are you *just* a doctor?"

My eyes searched his. What did he mean?

"You don't even have a master's?" he scoffed. And then he said what I shared with you before: "You should have waited to come when you had more qualifications. You could have done so much more for us."

As I considered the sacrifices I'd made and the surgical residency I'd relinquished to be there, my heart was singed with pain. Excusing myself shortly after, I ran home and wept.

Stained by humiliation, I knew this man was right. As a young doctor, my skills were limited, and the more I served the poor, the more I discovered my lack. A public health mentor back home in Singapore had told me, "The world's poor deserve the world's very best. You *need* to go to Johns Hopkins, Wai Jia. Forget about the online degree you're thinking of pursuing—you need to be there in person. In Baltimore."

Only Cliff knew how much those encounters shook me. "If you trust God with your dreams, He will sort things out," he would say, his broad arm around my shoulders. Although Cliff never spoke on behalf of God, never promised me God would fulfill all my dreams, a part of me lit up and died at the same time whenever I thought about Johns Hopkins. I wanted closure even if it meant letting my dream go.

But one day Cliff said, "It's time, Wai Jia." So for the third time, I began my application to Johns Hopkins for the Master of Public

Health program—but half-heartedly. I couldn't stand another disappointment. I lumbered through the onerous application, wondering if this might all be a waste of time. But at the end of each day, Cliff always reassured me, "Even if we don't know the final outcome, even if we don't know where God might lead us, our part is to take each step forward with Him."

One day he said, "Look here," then started by reciting his favorite Bible verse, Hebrews 11:8. "'By faith Abraham obeyed when he was called to go out to the place which he would receive as an inheritance. And he went out, not knowing where he was going.' Wai Jia, Abraham didn't know where his next stop would be, and God counted his faith as righteousness for following Him. So just keeping taking steps forward with God until He closes those doors."

The story of Abraham's sojourn begins in Genesis 12:1, where the Lord said to him (his name still Abram at the time), "Get out of your country, from your family and from your father's house, to a land that I will show you." When God called this man to leave all that was familiar to him, he obeyed at once. Even though he had no idea what Canaan was like—whether it was a good land or bad, and even though Canaanites were still living in Canaan at the time of God's call—he left, surrendering each step to God.

Imagine this. You've just been given an address for an important meeting God has set up for you. You have no idea where it is. What will you do? You'll probably jump into a car, cab, or bus, believing the driver will get you there. In the same way you would get to your destination that way, Abraham traveled to Canaan "by faith." We, too, can let our faith be the vehicle we embark to take us from where we are to where God wants us to be in the future.

In the same way, God often calls us into the unknown without revealing the answers to the many questions we might have. Even though Abraham would never live to see his offspring inherit the land, he went ahead and "built an altar" in Canaan, in an act of faith that the land would be his (Genesis 12:7).

When we go in faith and surrender each step to God, we build figurative "altars" of faith in our spiritual journeys. Our little steps forward matter to God.

The question I'd like to ask you today is this: Do you believe God has revealed a dream to you? If so, but the dream seems implausible or too far off in the future or requires too much sacrifice to leave your comfort zone into unknown territory, do you feel overwhelmed? God knows. Yet, like for Abraham, who traveled to an unknown land by faith, God wants us to jump into our vehicle of faith to take the next step forward.

I hope this next story of surrendering each step to God will encourage you to not be overwhelmed by how far and unknown the destination is but rather be encouraged that God always provides enough grace for our next step ahead.

Hold On to Your God-Given Glimpse of the Future

At an award ceremony I attended, an Afghan woman told of her father sending her to school against cultural norms. Protestors shot bullets into their doors to dissuade them. And then a bizarre thing happened. In my mind's eye, I saw a vision of me in Baltimore, Maryland, at Johns Hopkins.

I returned home, shaken. Although at first I thought about all the reasons I'd never get there (and I'll tell you more about that in the next chapter), the vision had lit a new hope within me. Day after day, every evening I'd plodded through that monstrous application before snuggling into Cliff's arms, heart heavy with unanswered questions. Would I be accepted? How would we pay for the tuition fees? Yet my husband maintained a firm calmness, assuring me that this blind following of God's gentle leading, even if it led to nothing, was right. Surrendering each step to God as I took baby steps of faith forward was good.

So imagine the betrayal I felt that day when Cliff returned from work at our church of five thousand people to tell me he'd been offered the opportunity to be the missions coordinator. What an honor—the job of his dreams! My heart swelled with pride for him. Yet I couldn't rejoice. What did this mean for *my* dream?

That night, forks clinked against dinnerware. We ate quietly, the air pregnant with tension. Our internal turmoil grew. Yet the more it grew, the more we prayed. As we were husband and wife, surely God had a common dream for us to grow toward, not separate ones to tear us apart. We pressed in, seeking Him for our next steps even though we didn't know where we were headed. And prayer did its painful work of piercing our hearts, untangling matted knots of pride and entitlement.

Slowly, I felt my dream of studying at Johns Hopkins slipping away like a kite caught in the wind. Perhaps it just was not meant to be, and it was time to let go.

We decided if God made it clear that Cliff should take up this leadership role in Singapore, I would give up my application to study at Johns Hopkins or at least do the program online part-time. We also decided if God made it clear that I should pursue a degree in America, then Cliff would give up his job offer in Singapore.

John 12:24 came to mind. Jesus said to His disciples—and of course says to all of us—"Unless a grain of wheat falls into the ground and dies, it remains alone; but if it dies, it produces much grain." God was asking Cliff and me to each lay our particular dreams to rest, however painful it might be, and trust that whatever He chose to resurrect would bear fruit that would last for His eternal glory. Through the work of enjoined, daily prayer, we decided pursuing our dreams would be about "us" in God, not about one or the other. If God had ordained for us to be as one, would He not grow us toward a joint dream that was bigger than the sum of us combined?

One evening, hearts heavy, we buried our individual dreams in an act of surrender.

I lay in bed that night, overcome by a new revelation. My dream was dead. I told the Lord I was through with my application. If He'd planned all these obstacles to prevent me from pursuing this dream, then I'd received the message. Like Hannah—who in 1 Samuel 1:10–11 was driven to desperation in waiting for a child and promised to give any child she would have back to God—I consecrated my dream of going to Baltimore to the Lord, promising I would give the degree however earned back to Him for the cause of missions.

The following days were hard. No matter how I tried to escape the vision God had given me at that award ceremony, I could not. *Perhaps I should pursue a degree locally. Maybe I could help Cliff in his pastoral role.* But whenever I looked over my shoulder, the only thing I could see was a gaping emptiness, the space in my life where my dream used to be.

Like Abraham did, I felt I was walking aimlessly. Would I ever reach this hoped-for destination? Scholarship opportunities opened up, but with tears, I put them aside. Cliff reminded me, though, "Until God has absolutely closed the door to Johns Hopkins, you should apply for the scholarships."

"There are so many of them, Cliff. I don't want to waste everyone's time. And they only cover on-campus studies. If you take up your job offer, none of these scholarships will matter."

"Apply to all of them. Remember your vision! Until God has spoken clearly, you should press on ahead. Just keep surrendering each step to Him."

In the Secret Place Comes True Surrender

One night, alone with God as Cliff slept, I punctured the dark canvas of night with pointed, questioning prayers. But He demanded a deeper surrender still. My energy drained away until my grudging anger melted into buttery yieldedness, and my clenched hands opened. I exchanged resentment for refreshment, self-centeredness for Spirit. My hands were finally empty, and I was ready to receive.

In the secret place comes true surrender.

Then asleep, I had a dream that I was flying a kite like the kite in *Kitesong*, my book about finding one's dreams. The string broke, and my kite came crashing down. I ran to it, picked it up, and raced to deliver it to Cliff. He turned to me and said, "I will help you fly it again."

I awoke, a tingly sensation all over me.

That week our senior pastor asked to meet Cliff and me. His staff had prepared Cliff's contract as missions coordinator, and I was asked to be present for the signing. My heart lurched. This meeting must be God's confirmation we should stay in Singapore.

The heels of my shoes dug deep into the carpet as I sat waiting for the announcement that would finally put an end to our uncertainty and a full stop to my dream. I had told the Lord if it was His will for me to serve Him without a higher degree—especially one earned in Baltimore—I was willing to surrender.

"Tell me what's been on your mind," my pastor said pointedly.

Cliff and I stared at each other, not knowing where to start. Awash with unease, the vision I had of me studying at Johns Hopkins in Baltimore reemerged. I had so much to say. But when the words reached my mouth, they were a stuttering, garbled mess.

My pastor cut me short. "All right. I wanted to let you both know that we were ready to take you on. We printed Cliff's contract yesterday. But as I gathered all the senior leaders together to pray this morning, we experienced a unanimous sense from the Holy Spirit that we have to release you to your original plans. God wants you overseas. This job offer may be open to Cliff at another season in his life, but this is the time you both need to go."

I sat there blinking, mouth open as my pulse hammered my temples. Then my eyes watched Cliff like a hawk's, searching for something that revealed his true emotions. The world seemed to hold still in a gasping pause.

Cliff finally spoke. "God's way is the best way. He has spoken. Let's celebrate!"

I looked at him in disbelief, but then said, "Our adventure begins!"

He laughed. "Thank God I told you to apply for those scholarships. Keep walking forward!"

The months after that seemed surreal as events played out as though in a storybook. Complex plots fell into the right places like puzzle pieces. Johns Hopkins accepted my application.

I'd given up on my dream of studying there in person, as I assumed that even if Cliff did not take the job in Singapore, we'd need to return to Canada for him to renew his residency status, ensuring continuity of his healthcare coverage. This was important for his transplant-related issues.

But then news of our pregnancy coincided with the start of the online program. That gave me the courage to convert my application for the online/part-time program to a deferred full-time/on-campus program. The timing of the start of the full-time program was uncanny. Not only did it give us ample time to visit Canada first to deliver our baby with Cliff's family close by, but it also gave us the exact duration of time needed to fulfill the minimum time requirement for Cliff's healthcare coverage to kick in.

Once again, everything aligned to a *T*. The Master of Public Health office agreed to all my requests. I lay in bed that night nearly paralyzed with gratitude for God's gentle guidance and perfect orchestration even amid confusion.

Through this experience, I learned how important it is to take the visions God gives us seriously and to persist through uncertainty. I learned our dreams belong to God. As with kites, if we hold on too tightly, the strings will break. But in the secret place of surrender and yielding, when we release our dreams to the One who created them, that's when we can truly see them soar.

God treasures His promises. Our dreams matter to Him. When it seems like they're too implausible or far away, when too many uncertainties stand between us and His "promised land," God doesn't want us to give up. He wants us to press in further and take steps of faith in surrender even if we may not know where we're going. Had I stopped short of my application earlier because I felt confused, had I ceased writing to scholarship boards because I saw no way out from our circumstances, those doors would have been closed forever.

And God wanted Cliff and me to press in further in prayer as individuals as well, to put to death our perceived individual rights and surrender each step to Him together. Had we decided to pursue our dreams individually, He would not have been able to do that deeper work in our marriage. While God is sovereign and His ways cannot be thwarted, He needs us to partner with Him in obedience, faith, and intercession. Such is the mystery of His ways.

So even when it seems like all is lost, when you're caught in a gale and your kite string breaks, know that in the secret place of surrender, you can find God. Even when you don't know where you're headed, His Word will be a lamp unto your feet, a guide for your path, leading you ahead one step at a time (Psalm 119:105). If it is truly His will, He will help you fly your kite again. He will guide you to your final destination. Just surrender each step to Him.

FOR REFLECTION

1. How do you think Abraham felt when God called him out from his homeland into Canaan?
2. How do you relate to Abraham in your own faith journey?
3. What kinds of uncertainties have you had to face that make surrendering your next steps to God challenging?

NEXT STEPS

1. Draw a simple map showing where you think you are with your dreams and where you feel God wants you to be. You may draw symbols representing your obstacles in between. Then draw yourself in your vehicle of faith and illustrate on the map where you think you'll next be.
2. What anxieties do you struggle with? Cup them in your hands, and in a symbolic act of faith, lift them up and give them to the Lord.
3. Spend some time in prayer. Although you may not know your future, what next step do you sense God is asking you to take? Write that down.

PRAYER

God, I know you have plans for me, yet it's hard for me to trust you fully—especially when I don't know the future. Just as Abraham had the faith to go out into the unknown, will you give me that same faith, the yieldedness to surrender each step forward to you? Grant me grace to trust you even when I'm overwhelmed and confused. As you have revealed your plans for my life to me, so shall they be. Amen.

13

build your ark of faith

> By faith Noah, being divinely warned of things not yet seen, moved with godly fear, prepared an ark for the saving of his household, by which he condemned the world and became heir of the righteousness which is according to faith.
>
> —Hebrews 11:7

ALTHOUGH THAT VISION of me studying public health at Johns Hopkins later lit a hope in me, my lips mouthed the words *I can't*. It was too far away. Too hard. Our circumstances wouldn't allow it.

The endeavor was just too expensive.

The tuition fees of over a hundred thousand dollars were staggering. And my compulsory bond with the government had not yet been completed, so why would they grant me no-pay leave again, especially after I'd taken a year off to serve in Uganda? My poor grades in medical school due to my bout with anorexia and depression would surely disqualify me from any scholarships.

After all, I'd been hearing things like, "There are many good options for further studies locally, Wai Jia," and "You can just study the Johns Hopkins course online. Think about the money you would save!"

Do you, like I did, find yourself vacillating between two extremes? One day feeling zealous for the dreams God has revealed to you and another day feeling overwhelmed with fear by naysayers (even yourself) and the obstacles ahead? You are not alone. Hebrews 11:7 says, "By faith Noah, being divinely warned of things not yet seen, moved with godly fear, prepared an ark for the saving of his household, by which he condemned the world and became heir of the righteousness which is according to faith."

The Bible doesn't say, but as Noah prepared the ark, he most likely faced ridicule and scorn—even self-doubt. Can you imagine he might have thought, *Did I hear God correctly? What if I can't build the ark successfully? What if there's no flood? If there is, what if the ark sinks?* But he didn't let any of that stop him. Instead, he was "moved with godly fear"—which in the Greek refers not to a slavish kind of fear but a "reverential fear"—to complete the job God had tasked him to do.[1] Amid the world's likely sneering disbelief, he plowed on in faith, not only saving his household but becoming an "heir of righteousness."

The truth is this: when we pursue God's dreams for our lives, people will mock us. Challenges may seem insurmountable. But when we commit to what God has called us to and resist being overwhelmed by the mammoth-sized task ahead of us, our faith becomes the ark that buoys our family and future generations and invites us into sonship as heirs of Christ.[2]

In this chapter, I share the story about how I ignored the resounding voice of *I can't* to build my ark of faith, which unleashed God's provision of over a hundred thousand dollars to fund our journey to America and back. I hope it will encourage you to not be discouraged by the incredulity of your dreams but to dig deep and commit to building your ark every day. After all, God has the blueprint. All we need is, like Noah, to dig in and dig deep, trust and obey.

Impossible Situations Are Invitations for God to Enter In

Even though my hope had been renewed by the vision God gave me about Johns Hopkins, the more I thought about it, the more it really did seem impossible.

One day while attending a health equity conference, something else bizarre happened. A petite, blond, older American lady with rouge lipstick, also an attendee, followed me wherever I went.

"May I sit with you?" she said in the conference hall.

Thereafter, she never left me. And when the audience broke off into groups for panel discussions in various breakout rooms, she trailed me, saying, "I'd love to go where you're going." Even at lunchtime, she made herself my designated lunch buddy.

"What are your dreams?" she asked, quizzing me about my career goals.

I held back at first. After all, she was a stranger. Why burden her with my life's aspirations and problems? Yet I felt a certain resonance with her, a strange peace.

That evening over dinner, I told Cliff, "I don't know how to explain this—you'll probably think I'm mad—but I've never felt like that with a stranger before. It's like I sense she's an angel or something. Our conversations have seemed so God-sent. I don't know what God's up to, but I'm sensing something supernatural."

The next day, the same thing happened. This lady with red lipstick and blond hair trailed me wherever I went. "So what do you dream of doing in your next few years?" she asked.

Finally, careful to hold back tears, I shared, "My dream is to study public health at Johns Hopkins and to use what I learn to serve the poor. But I don't know if I'll qualify for any scholarships, and without them, there's no way I could go there." And then I blurted, "Why are you taking such an interest in my life?"

I saw a veiled amusement in her face, and I sat in rapt attention, slightly petrified she would tell me she was an angelic being in human form. What would I say to that?

"I'm the dean of a medical university in Texas," she said. "I'm actually a Fulbright Scholar on a fellowship in Singapore."

I breathed a sigh of quiet relief knowing she was a real human being!

Then she added, "You have to send me your résumé, okay?"

The series of divinely orchestrated events that ensued after, of which the Fulbright Program played a central role, often make me wonder if those initial bizarre feelings were inklings of God at work, of showing me that this woman was indeed sent by Him.

Little did I know that Fulbright's was one of the most prestigious scholarships in the world, and I certainly didn't know it was available to post-graduate students in Singapore. "You have to apply so you can attend Johns Hopkins in Baltimore," my new friend said. She was insistent.

"But I can't," I told her, arguing before heaving a sigh of despair. For one thing, at the time I'd applied for the Johns Hopkins online program, not for the one onsite, and most scholarships don't cover online programs. And my no-pay leave would likely not be approved anyway. Also, if Cliff didn't take up the job offer in Singapore, we'd have to head to Canada to renew his residential status to ensure continued healthcare coverage for his liver transplant. How could I attend an interview for a Fulbright scholarship in person if it came about while we were there?

As if God knew I needed a persistent American dean of an established medical school in Texas to trail me around for two days and then egg me on to see a Fulbright scholarship application to completion, this lady emailed me every week in the months after to ensure I'd put my application in no matter how uncertain I felt about my future. Without my knowing or understanding, she was helping me build my ark.

God Works in Unexpected Ways

Soon after, Cliff and I discovered I was pregnant, and Johns Hopkins allowed me to convert my online program to their onsite program in Baltimore.

The day for the Fulbright interview came, and I milled outside the Singapore United States embassy, my heart in my throat. The building, made of a dark-gray stone, was tall and forbidding and sat atop a slope in the city. My stomach felt light and fluttery.

Just outside the interview room sat rows of outstanding candidates, bristling with brilliance. Why did I think I even stood a chance? My university transcripts were filled with Bs and Cs. Because of the depression and anorexia I'd experienced, I'd struggled to even graduate from medical school.

To my chagrin, a young man, bright and eager, thought making small talk before a life-changing interview might help ease nerves.

"What's your name?"

"What do you do?"

"What are you applying for?"

He was thrilled to find a fellow doctor. I wanted to curtail the conversation but felt obligated to at least politely return the questions.

"Oh, I'm applying for an MBA from Harvard," he told me. "I thought of doing an MPH at Johns Hopkins, but after thinking about it, I decided that degree is *bloody useless!*"

His emphasis on the last two words rattled me. My hands felt cold and clammy.

During the interview, my heart pounded in my chest. Those two words kept replaying in my mind as I shared why I'd chosen to pursue this degree. The room was large and spacious, but a claustrophobic feeling pressed into my forehead—everything seemed too small, too tight. Finally, when I shared that I was pregnant and would deliver our baby just before the program started, I was sure I'd squandered my opportunity. Someone like that guy in the reception area—sharp, brilliant, and witty—was probably who they were looking for.

"We will inform you of our decision in a month."

I stood, my heart sinking to the floor.

I emerged from the air-conditioned cool of the embassy building into the harsh sunlight outside, stunned and embarrassed, my pulse still thumping in my head, walking fast so I wouldn't retch. I'd never felt so nervous, so afraid, as if so much of my life depended on that one interview.

Six days later, I awoke from a dream, its details freshly embroidered in my mind. I'd received an envelope embossed with a red seal, and when I opened it, I found a letter from the Fulbright scholarship board with the words *You have been accepted* underlined in red ink.

The next day, I received a phone call. "Congratulations, Dr. Tam. From the dozens of applicants who interviewed, you're one of the two selected to be a Fulbright scholar."

Weeks later, when the Fulbright Scholarship Board invited me to the American Embassy to officially award the two awardees the scholarship, I learned that the other scholar was "Mister Harvard!" God spoke to me, saying that while we might compare ourselves to others and feel grossly incapable, His grace and favor can cover our perceived inadequacies. If God has a plan, no man can thwart it.

From the previous chapter, you know the rest of the tailspin. Shortly after this, our senior pastor retracted Cliff's job offer in Singapore and encouraged us to head overseas.

A week before our departure for Canada, where I would give birth, I was informed that my request for no-pay leave, which had been forwarded to the parliamentary level, had been approved for not one but two years, covering not only the length of my studies but Cliff's residential status and healthcare renewal in Canada and my maternity leave. With the Fulbright scholarship, and a supplementary scholarship from Johns Hopkins, about half of my tuition fees was covered.

Yet the other half still needed to be raised.

As the days went by, my hope for the financial assistance we still needed grated thin. But I thought back on the countless opportunities God had provided for us and felt led to pray. If He could provide for half of our expenses, could He not raise the remaining half?

Often, I thought of Noah building the ark and wondered if he ever stopped midway, taken aback by the enormity of the task ahead, and doubted what God had asked him to do. At three hundred cubits long and thirty cubits high, the ark was nearly one and a half football fields long and bigger than a modern four-story house (Genesis 6:15).[3] But the Bible gives us no clue that Noah ever wavered, just that he "did according to all that the LORD commanded him" (Genesis 7:5).

I thought if I could put all my financial anxieties into prayer and what God told me to do day by day, I could press on. So instead of worrying, I asked God what He would have me do each day. Whether it was praying, writing letters to share our prayer requests, or filling in applications for potential scholarships, like Noah, I busied myself in building my ark.

One scholarship board I had yet to hear from promised grants of limited amounts. Their website clearly stated, "We usually provide grants of up to $15,000." With the exchange rate, that amount was a drop in the bucket, and I would still be short 40 percent of my tuition and living expenses. And now being overseas in Canada to deliver our firstborn meant I couldn't attend the scholarship interview in person. That would significantly diminish my chance of success.

Yet I began to sow into that mustard seed of faith, asking God to provide for our young family. Like Noah, I dug in and dug deep, putting all my energy into prayer.

Then came a flurry of emails and a much-anticipated Skype meeting with the scholarship board. I sat in our tiny matchbox living room in Canada with a tender, postpartum body, nervously waiting for an interview in a time zone twelve hours away in Singapore. Cliff sneaked out the door quietly to drive our newborn in circles around the neighborhood so I could be interviewed uninterrupted.

Two weeks later I received an email from the board. I steadied my heart, unsure of what to expect. But as soon as I read it, I stormed into the bedroom ranting, "Oh my goodness, Cliff! I'm so happy I got the scholarship, but I feel emotionally *cheated.* How unprofessional! How could they misprint an extra zero in the offer letter?"

I wrote back to the scholarship board immediately, requesting a clarification of what seemed to be a grave error. Surely they meant to say I'd received a grant of $10,000 and pocket money of $5,000. That was the usual limit stated on their website. How could they mistype their letter?

But there was no mistake. "Dear Dr. Tam, our Board has decided to award you a total of $60,000 comprising a grant of $10,000 and pocket money of $50,000 to support you in your further studies. There is no mistake."

Together with the other two scholarships, the full cost of my tuition at Johns Hopkins was covered. Then weeks later, we received an anonymous love gift of $40,000 through a friend, specifying it was to cover living expenses for our family of three during the years we were overseas.

Even when all hope had seemed lost, when all possibility of my studying at Johns Hopkins in Baltimore had seemed at least stretched thin, the obstacles in the way collapsed one by one like dominoes. I learned that when it seems like our dreams are impossible to reach, it's crucial to walk with God and obey what He tells us to do, even when we don't understand why.

Had Noah not pressed on to finish the ark, even when the task seemed like a tall order and he was the object of ridicule, he would not have lived this amazing testimony of faith. Had I not reapplied at Johns Hopkins, had I not recognized that meeting that dean at the conference was a divine setup, had I not applied for scholarships even when Cliff had been offered a job in Singapore and we didn't know which path God would choose for us, had I not continued to build my ark, none of this would have happened.

This is what God needs from us—to build our arks in faith even when we don't understand, even when our hope wears thin.

It baffles me to think about how all this could happen to someone who floundered through medical school. Back then, I wasn't even sure if I would graduate on time—or at all. It baffles me to think that all three scholarship boards were willing to take a risk on a mama with a newborn—what a risk! What undeserved grace I'd received.

God made the impossible, possible.

When we pursue God's dreams for our lives, the tasks may seem incredulous. Yet perhaps we need to remember it is precisely because our dreams are God-breathed that we need God's intervention. Noah didn't allow what people might think of him, or any self-doubts about "things not yet seen," or the immensity of his task to stop him from building the ark.

Likewise, we must ignore the resounding voice of *I can't* to build our arks of faith through prayer. I truly believe it was faith in our big God, however shaky, that unleashed His provision of over a hundred thousand dollars to make this dream of studying at Johns Hopkins come true. Like Noah, all we need to do is obey. After all, like in the building of the ark, God already knows the outcome. He has the blueprint in His hands (Genesis 6:14–16)!

Make no mistake, the cost of failing to trust God is high. Just as how Noah saved an entire generation and beyond, our walking in obedience with Christ builds a faith that sows into generations beyond us. *That* is what's at stake.

Hebrews 3:15 tells us, "Today, if you will hear His voice, do not harden your hearts as in the rebellion." Has God revealed a glimpse of His blueprint for your life? Do you think it impossible for your dream to be fulfilled, for complex things to fall into place? Through prayer and taking small steps forward, keep building your ark of faith. For when it is complete, only then will you see the legacy you've reaped not only for yourself but for your family and generations to come.

FOR REFLECTION

1. Have you ever felt overwhelmed by the magnitude of what God has called you to? If so, how did you cope?
2. In times of discouragement or scorn from others, how can you best respond?
3. How can you maintain a posture of faith and trust even in the face of "things not yet seen"?

NEXT STEPS

1. What glimpse of God's blueprint for your life has He revealed to you so you can complete the building of your ark? Write that down.
2. Like Noah, into what "baby steps" can you break your "big task"? Just as how Noah must have delegated the work and focused on building a little of the ark each day, what "little tasks" and/or prayer habits can you focus on each day to build your ark daily? Write them down.
3. Imagine your spiritual ark of faith successfully built. What eternal rewards are sown into your family's future generations? Close your eyes in prayer and ask the Lord to reveal them to you. Then write them down.

PRAYER

God, building an ark of faith is never easy. Yet just as how Noah was determined, I desire to commit to the task you've called me to and work at it with an unwavering faith. Come what may, grant me the doggedness to work on the dream you have called me to each day, trusting that your blueprint is sure. Let me, like Noah, build an ark of faith that will impact future generations for years to come. Amen.

14

push past your doubt

> By faith Sarah herself also received strength to conceive seed, and she bore a child when she was past the age, because she judged Him faithful who had promised.
>
> —Hebrews 11:11

WHENEVER I LET ON that I'd had a drug-free home birth for both my children, I watch the reactions of others with carefully concealed amusement.

"You what? Didn't the pain kill you?"

"That's crazy! How is that even possible?"

"You're a doctor. Why didn't you do it in a hospital?"

Growing up, I never imagined having a home birth. After all, home births are almost unheard of in Singapore. Labor is typically seen as a critically dangerous event in a woman's life best observed in a hospital under the watchful eye of professionals and the beeping rhythm of monitoring machines. Labor looked excruciating on television shows, and the plethora of drugs and interventions we'd learned about in medical school to alleviate its suffering only attested to its poor reputation. Having assisted with several complicated deliveries at hospitals, the myriad of unfortunate outcomes of labor had etched themselves deeply on me.

So I understand why most people find it nearly impossible to wrap their heads around the idea of a drug-free, natural birth in the comforts of home. But my decision had nothing to do with how high my pain threshold is or how brave I am. It's far simpler than that.

As that eighteen-year-old girl welcomed into the children's home in Nepal, I spent evenings huddled with others around a coal stove, listening to the missionary houseparents' stories. One sent us all into stitches and tears of laughter.

The missionary mother of three said, "I could have had our baby in Singapore or India. But God told us to stay here in Nepal where He called us to serve. But thank God, Baby slipped out so fast that the nurses were telling me to hold on! They laid me on a metal trolley, no mattress, and soon after I delivered, they sent me walking upstairs by myself, holding my own IV drip."

We roared with incredulity and amusement.

Yet that story sowed a seed of faith in me. Later in life, I met an American pastor's wife who had two beautiful home births, and that sealed my decision to do the same even if I didn't know how. I wanted to know for myself that, should I have a baby in the mission field in the future, no matter where in the world that might be, I would have the faith to deliver our baby, no matter what the circumstances might be.

So with my first pregnancy, I hoped I would be strong enough to undergo a drug-free, natural home birth.

Hebrews 11:11 says, "By faith Sarah herself also received strength to conceive seed, and she bore a child when she was past the age, because she judged Him faithful who had promised." This refers to Abraham's wife, Sarah, who, when God promised them a son, laughed and said, "Shall I surely bear a child, since I am old?" (Genesis 18:13).

At the time, Sarah was way past her childbearing years. Earlier, weary of waiting for a child, she'd suggested her husband sleep with her maid to produce an heir for him to fulfill God's promise (Genesis 16:2). By taking the situation into her own hands, Ishmael was born. And sadly, conflicts between Ishmael's and Isaac's lines have affected generations ever since.[1]

Yet despite all the above, Hebrews 11:11 commends Sarah for her faith. Here, we see how her initial doubts didn't discount her from receiving God's promises.[2] Rather, her subsequent faith in God gave her strength to conceive even in circumstances that seemed impossible.

This encourages us that our doubts don't discount us from fulfilling God's dreams for us. Rather, as we press in, our faith can supersede our unbelief and cause our spiritual wombs, even if once barren, to bear fruit.

The very name of Abraham and Sarah's child together, Isaac, which means "laughter" and refers to Sarah's initial disbelief at God's promise of a natural-born child in their old age, also indicates the joy with which they welcomed their breakthrough. Thus, our unbelief can even bear witness to the faith that supersedes it.

I hope the following lessons I gleaned from my home births in a land away from home will encourage you to push past moments of unbelief and discomfort, to conceive and birth God's amazing miracles and dreams for your life.

Trust the Birth Process

The moment we decided to have a home birth, I sensed God whisper to my heart, *Trust Me. This will be a physical experience to remember but also a spiritual one. I will guide and lead you.*

It would have been incredibly difficult to find a home-birth option in Singapore. But as God would have it, because of the timing of my no-pay leave and start date for my studies at Johns

Hopkins, we were led to move to Canada, where Cliff's parents lived, not long before my due date. Only God could have planned it better—to send me to a land where home births were not only far more commonplace but highly coveted.

Yet a Canadian friend of Cliff's warned me with good intentions. "Oh, you won't be able to find a midwife in time, Wai Jia. People book them the moment they discover their pregnancies. You're in your third trimester, and you won't stand a chance. Just don't be disappointed."

But I emailed dozens of midwives anyway. If God had spoken to me about this, about a specific spiritual experience He was preparing for me, would He not make it happen?

Just weeks before we moved to Canada, I received this email: *I watched the viral love story you shared over email. Although I'm fully booked up, I've now become the director of my own midwifery practice, and so I'm taking you in as my personal client.*[3]

I looked at the email, heart surging with gratitude as faith filled my being. Yet as the birth neared, I developed cold feet. A family doctor we'd visited for a cold had shaken his head gravely. Tsking, he chided, "You guys don't know what you're doing. Labor hurts like hell! Don't you have the sense to go to hospital for your first birth? Get your epidural early! What if something bad happens? Have you never seen a baby being strangled by its own umbilical cord? You'll be too far from the hospital by then."

I stared at the doctor, shaken. The Lord's gentle whisper continued to speak to me—*Trust Me*—yet like Sarai, I struggled with doubt. *Perhaps I should convert to a hospital birth?* But God's gentle nudging reassured me. *I provided your midwife. I am in control.*

To prepare myself, I read about natural births, and what I learned blew my mind. What stood out most to me was the profound impact a mother's mindset toward pain has on her birth experience. By embracing her pain, by surrendering the outcome to a higher power, and by trusting in the natural birth process itself, the perceived pain of labor can be significantly reduced.

In contrast, if a mother fears labor, resents pain, and doubts her body's ability to give birth to her child, escalating interventions tend to follow. One particular stage of natural labor caught my attention. Close to actual birth, the "transition stage" is the point where contractions pile up one over another and the pain becomes overwhelming, giving way to an inexorable desire to push and birth something glorious.[4] Yet it's also infamously marked by the mother's fatigue, self-doubt, and desire to give up even though this stage is very close to birth.

In your journey to birthing the dreams God has placed in you, do you experience doubt and fear? Like Sarai, do you wonder how your dreams in your younger days could come to pass at this stage of your life? Do you experience fear that what God might put you through could be too much to bear?

Like in the labor of childbirth, I learned that God calls us to embrace pain and trust that He has created us to be sufficient for the dream-birthing process. Though it may be painful and push our limits, we have the capacity to stretch and birth His purposes.

When You're Stuck, Push Through

Contractions began in the early morning. Then after a day of walking around malls and even hiking knee-deep in snow at a park, we returned home. To Cliff's amusement, I cooked dinner and cleaned the house before finally admitting it was time to call our midwife, Barb.

Soon a wave of pain hit me like a ton of bricks. Another came—and another. Eventually, all the waves combined into gigantic tsunamis that crashed over me. Then I hit a mental wall. No amount of pushing was making progress. I strained and pushed and squeezed, but the baby was stuck. I envisioned myself strong and persevering, but my determination leaked away. To my horror, I whimpered to Cliff, "I can't do this anymore. I'm done."

Doubt, fear, and anxiety all took over. The words of our family doctor rang clear in my head. Perhaps this *was* all a big mistake. Perhaps he was right after all, that a woman's first labor should happen at a hospital. The faith I had so firmly held on to fell through my fingers like sand.

Then Barb said, "Wai Jia, your baby is stuck at a sticky point. If you don't push past it, we'll have to do a hospital transfer."

"Gosh," I said, my face flushed with heat. "How many pushes do you think I need?"

"Twenty. Twenty *good* ones."

"Twenty!" I gasped, nearly crying.

Cliff held me, rubbing his hands hard on my back. "Oh Lord," he prayed, "we need you!"

As he said that, our baby began to crown, and with just *one* final, focused push, Sarah-Faith slipped out, wet like a fish, and in one full sweep from womb to breast she took her first breath of air.

I now recognize that moment of desperation as the "transition stage," marked as the woman's most vulnerable, most intense, most difficult stage of labor. Journals record that women are "especially vulnerable to suggestion at this time, which can be used to enhance or hinder the birth."[5]

Similarly, in our dream journeys, many of us will inevitably face our own "sticky points" where we feel overwhelmed by doubt and fear. We may think we've made a mistake, that perhaps it would have been better to back out earlier. Yet precisely at this point is when the mother is incredibly close to birth and needs to push past those doubts. And so do we when we face our own.

Hebrews 11:11 assures us that despite our initial unbelief, our subsequent faith in God can supersede our initial faltering and mark us for life.

If you're called to a unique destiny, God may call you to do things that are different, that others will naturally discourage you from doing even if they have the best intentions. After all, my family doctor was only concerned! If Sarah and Abraham had shared God's promise to them with their friends, imagine what the naysayers would have said.

"How can that be possible?"

"Oh, but you're so old. Labor could be dangerous!"

"You'll be such old parents that you won't have the energy to raise a baby well."

Yet at the end of our lives, each of us are accountable only to God, not to anyone else. Your destiny is preordained from the beginning of time by your heavenly Father, and it'll fall right in place with your heart's calling if you stay true to who you are and what you've been called to (Ephesians 2:10). Don't let doubts at your "transition stage" disarm you. Don't let pain veer you off-course. Pain is part of the journey.

Lean into Your Pain to Birth Something Glorious

If we thought our first labor was quick, our second, also in Canada, happened at full tilt.

At lunchtime, Cliff took a look at me and said, "I should call Barb now."

"Just relax," I told him, looking for a bottle of sweet Thai chili sauce to polish off my spring roll. "Let's not waste Barb's time by making her come too early."

Our firstborn, Sarah-Faith, a rambunctious two-year-old by then, tugged at me, pointing to her book on the floor. But then a contraction came, throwing me onto my hands and knees. Oblivious to the drama about to unfold, our daughter cried out, "Mama! Read!"

Cliff jumped into action. "I'm calling Barb now!"

Minutes later, Barb waltzed in. As the contractions piled continuously on one another, I staggered at how frighteningly quick the pain intensified, far more quickly than for Sarah-Faith's birth. "If it's this intense now," I said, "I don't know how I'll make it through to the end."

Petrified, I began to shake. But as the contractions surged on, I did something new. During my first birth, whenever pain came, I lurched and resisted it. But this time I embraced and leaned into pain. During my struggle with depression after Sarah-Faith's birth and during this second pregnancy, the Lord had spoken to me daily, *Lean into your pain. As you lean in, your pain will birth something glorious.* Little did I realize how this could apply so aptly to the process of labor too.

With every wave of pain that came, I imagined myself leaning into it and letting its waves crash over me. This was counterintuitive, but it worked because the pain that overwhelmed me, that felt so scary like it was out to destroy me, was the very pain needed to bring the baby to birth.

So often we're that close to receiving our breakthrough. But we waver, we falter, not realizing that the length of our struggle doesn't determine the probability or nearness of our breakthrough. Like Sarai, we might be overwhelmed by doubt and be tempted to take things into our own hands. Yet if we trust that God has permitted the pain in our lives for a purpose He wants us to embrace, will we not come to enjoy the great reward born out of our deepest, most desperate cries?

Don't give up. Lean in. Push past your doubts.

Once I surrendered to the pain, Esther-Praise slipped out, all pink. On my knees, holding her, I both cried and laughed, not realizing how this intense labor reflects our journeying through the fulfilment of God's promises—filled with doubt, pain, and surrender but also glorious God-filled hope at the end.

All it took was a grand total of four minutes of pushing compared to three hours of active labor for my first birth. No sooner had the midwife's young assistant arrived than was she encouraged to leave because it was all over. She stepped in harried and frazzled to take a few family photos, profusely apologizing for arriving late, and congratulated us on her way out.

Minutes later, I learned that despite the speed of the labor, I didn't suffer any tears or require any stitches. I remember reading somewhere that serious perineal and vaginal tears can happen when one strains too hard or resists the contractions. Likewise, when we fight the pain allowed in our lives and strain against it, we can create serious collateral damage that can take even longer to heal than the length of time we experienced the pain.

In life, we cannot avoid pain. But we can choose the kind of pain we want to endure. What we choose determines the lessons we glean and take away, *so choose your pain wisely*. Embrace, and don't resist, the pain God has ordained for your life.

The fact is our determination to push through doubt and endure hardship to birth something glorious grows us into deeper maturity. In contrast, running away from God, as Jonah did, can not only prolong our pain but injure ourselves and our loved ones.

If you're facing pain this season, trust God. Hold on through your "transition stage." Push past your doubt. Lean into the pain. Transition is temporary. What will last for eternity, however, is the faith wrought through crisis as you lean into the Lord's bosom through it all.

When you feel like giving up the dreams God gave you, know that your breakthrough could be just around the corner. Your doubt may be great, but let your faith be greater still. Lean in. Dig deep. Don't let anyone say you can't because it's difficult or "hell." Determine first if it's what God has promised, and if it is, like Sarah, you can "judge Him faithful who had promised."

Then may your eyes, like mine were, be filled with tears of joy when you birth your glorious reward. May you, like Sarah, laugh at God's goodness. May you reap in joy what you sowed in tears.

FOR REFLECTION

1. What kinds of doubts have you experienced in your faith journey?
2. What makes you feel like giving up?
3. What keeps you going?

NEXT STEPS

1. As you bring your fears before God, repent of any doubts you may have toward His promises for your life.
2. As you pray, what is God showing you about your faith journey? Write down or draw these downloads.
3. What lessons have you gleaned from pushing past your doubt and leaning into pain? Write them down.

PRAYER

God, you know I wrestle with doubt, and sometimes I feel like giving up. I need a breakthrough! When unbelief assails me, will you help me push past doubt and lean into pain? Let my life, like Sarah's, be marked by faith, not doubt. Let my mouth, like Sarah's, be filled with laughter. Let me, by faith, birth your glorious dreams for my life. I trust that my faith will supersede all my doubts and leave behind a lasting legacy for generations to come. Amen.

15

wrestle with God

> By faith Jacob, when he was dying, blessed each of the sons of Joseph, and worshiped, leaning on the top of his staff.
>
> —Hebrews 11:21

"It's no use, Cliff!"

I'd come home from school and was now tearing up in my husband's arms. "We've come all the way from Singapore so I could attend Johns Hopkins, and now it's all been a waste. What am I here for?"

Day after day I'd scoured the faculty list at Johns Hopkins, writing to world-renowned professors asking if they would mentor me toward completion of my capstone project—whatever that would turn out to be. Like a child eager to win a prize, I was frantically thinking, *Pick me! Pick me!*

Before each meeting, I'd research the professor's area of specialty, hoping to present myself as the perfect mentee with a passionate interest in it. I'd take deep breaths, praying hard. Sometimes I felt like someone about to audition in a theater, rehearsing my script, desperate to be selected. But none of them picked me. So as more of my classmates landed big projects with the United

Nations, World Health Organization, and other large international nonprofits, I wrote to more professors, resolute to leave no stone unturned. After all, it would just be a matter of time before someone picked me as their mentee, willing to help me kickstart an illustrious public health career—right?

I admit, very shamefully, that despite all God had done to bring us to Baltimore, even providing enough for Cliff to be a stay-at-home dad there, I was determined to prove myself now without troubling Him. Now that God had done His part, surely it was time for me to do mine. And so, with this self-striving approach, I set my mind to network well and work hard, to land myself a prestigious project to bring that little dream I'd written on my medical school application when I was seventeen years old to pass. The one about serving the poor with the United Nations or the World Health Organization.

Weeks turned into months, and my supervisor gently reminded me, "If you don't find a mentor and a capstone project, you won't graduate."

My hopes began to fray.

Worse, when I walked into class one day, one of my classmates excitedly shouted, "Hey, you're the *Kitesong* girl! We found your books online. You're so gifted!" I wanted to bury my head in sand. I'd spent months trying to portray myself as a credible public health leader, and I'd been successful keeping *Kitesong* under wraps. No way was I going to let others think of me as a "fluffy" picture book illustrator! But now I was found out. What would others think of me?

One day I sensed God telling me, *Set aside Sundays for prayer. Do not work at all. Trust Me.*

I argued with Him. Most of my classmates were single and didn't have the responsibility of looking after a child, but even so they struggled with completing class assignments and studying for exams. I, of all people, did not have the luxury of wasting away an entire day of the week!

Yet God made His desire clear to me. *Devote Sundays to Me. Travail in prayer. In the secret place, I will show you your next steps.*

So on Sundays I closed myself off in our walk-in closet and prayed on my knees for hours. I remembered how Jacob, his name meaning "usurper" in Hebrew, wrestled with an angel till daybreak. During the struggle, the angel touched Jacob's hip socket till it was out of joint. Even then, Jacob didn't let up but said, "I will not let You go unless You bless me!" (Genesis 32:26).

Finally, through that wrestling encounter, Jacob was renamed Israel, meaning "prince of peace." Through that wrestling, he gained internal transformation and a new identity. And in that prayer closet, I developed Jacob's tenacity to hold on to God. "I will not let you go until you show me my next steps and bless me!" I cried.

As I pressed into God, something in me shifted. My position of petulance and striving gave way to a posture of prayer and humility. Hebrews 11:21 tells us that before Jacob died, by faith he "blessed each of the sons of Joseph, and worshiped, leaning on the top of his staff." A reflection of complete yieldedness to God.

What a stark contrast to the Jacob of self-striving before! Even though he would not see his descendants take hold of the promised land, his faith was exemplified in his continuation of passing down the blessings, as his fathers had, despite any self-doubts.[1] His leaning on his staff, an emblem of his pilgrim state on his way to his heavenly city, depicted his posture of dependance on God (Genesis 32:10).[2]

Let me share my own journey of learning to yield to God's ways, as Jacob did. I hope it will encourage you to wrestle with God in prayer and yield to Him until you receive your breakthrough.

In the Wrestling Ring of Prayer

One afternoon, during a last-ditch effort to land a capstone project with an infectious disease specialist, I told myself, *Any project will do as long as I can graduate!*

For the first time, I'd printed out my résumé, and after a quick glance at it, the specialist cast it back to me across the table dramatically. I stared at him, stunned.

"There's something else you really want," he said. "It's not this. I mean, look at your resume. What you want is written all over here. So tell me, when you search deep inside, what is it?"

Against my own wishes, words tumbled out. "I want to start an international nonprofit of sorts, using the power of storytelling, my books, to help the poor. I don't know how, but . . ."

What was I doing? I'd shot myself in the foot.

"That's your capstone project right there."

I flew out of his office, tears streaming as I ran to my supervisor's office. "Dr. Ann!" I knocked on her open door, oblivious of decorum. "I know what to do! Will you mentor me?"

A benevolent smile broke out across her face, and even before she knew what it was, she said, "Yes. I knew you would find it."

Yet I had not fully repented of self-striving. I threw myself into a frenzy of work, trying to make up for lost time. But then one day Cliff found me in a puddle of tears from sheer exhaustion. I felt like a blind man groping in the dark. But there, in the secret place of desperate prayer and angry questions, God began to reveal His hidden riches of secret places (Isaiah 45:3). As I came to the end of myself, God was waiting for me.

Keep consecrating your Sundays to Me, I sensed Him saying. But how could I? I was enrolled in an intense Master of Public Health course, a program that normally takes two years of full-time study elsewhere but is compressed into ten months at Johns Hopkins. A classmate confessed, "Sabbath is impossible here."

One Sunday I escaped to the gym, longing for distraction. I started listening to a sermon and found myself arrested by a message on the Tower of Babel. A vision of a tall tower of my own pride stood before me. Below it, throngs of people babbled. There on the StairMaster, the Holy Spirit overshadowed me. At once, I was naked and ashamed at my own striving. My knees felt weak, but God gripped me like a fierce hug.

The sermon progressed to describe the day of Pentecost as an event of restoration, and I saw a vision of my picture books traveling to different parts of the world, to people of different tongues. As they read the books, they started to praise the Lord in different languages.

How can this be, Lord? The books are in English.

The vision of the tower loomed over me. It swayed ominously, then crumbled. God spoke to me, *Every Sunday, I want you to wrestle in the place of prayer with Me.*

The restitution of Sabbath became a new cornerstone, the setting of a new foundation built on guttural groanings of faith. *From a posture of rest will come your miracle,* I felt God say. *Doing less is more.*

Our walk-in closet became a wrestling ring, a sanctuary of prayer. Six days later, a stranger from Singapore wrote to me:

> *I have been following your blog for years and have always felt God asking me to translate your picture books. But I could not find the courage to contact you. This weekend, God gave me a burden so heavy that I had no choice but to write to you. I would like to translate your books into Japanese and Tetum, so those communities may know His love.*

In the next three months, without any advertising, seven different people heeded the prompting of the Holy Spirit and stepped forward to translate the books into seven languages, fulfilling a glimpse of the vision I had for them to be a channel of God's blessing to the underserved.

Prayer Is the Work

Sundays in prayer became a necessity.

I began to pray for a team to start an international nonprofit ministry called Kitesong Global and specifically for a millennial to help me with a website. Two weeks later, a friend asked me for help hosting a Singaporean for lunch in Baltimore. I sat in the café, expecting a tall, middle-aged working man. Instead, a slight twenty-four-year-old art student showed up.

"I'm a graphic designer," he told me. "I feel God led me to you because He wants me to create your website. I won't charge you a cent."

I sat there, stunned, feeling God whisper, *Prayer is the work.*

During my time of prayer on Sundays, I felt an increasing burden to share about God's goodness in my life with my community at school. I remembered a Christian professor I'd met even before the term started, who had prophesied to me, "Your little baby Sarah-Faith will be an evangelist to our community."

As I prayed, an idea began to form. What if I launched Kitesong Global during a celebration of Sarah-Faith's first birthday? Over the months, as she'd regularly accompanied me to lectures and classes, my daughter had become an iconic baby at school. Many people endearingly called her the school mascot and often started conversations with me because of her presence. The occasion could be a platform to share God's testimonies in my life with my friends. But how would I make that happen?

One afternoon I bumped into my program director along the corridor.

"I was wondering if, for Sarah-Faith's birthday, I could do a personal sharing in a small classroom and launch Kitesong Global as well."

She smiled. "For an occasion such as this, we'll need a far better venue than that!"

The next day, the program office's staff informed me that instead of a small classroom, they'd booked the largest function hall at Johns Hopkins and had sent an email to all school clubs and associations asking them not to organize any clashing events. The Kitesong Global launch was announced as an official school-wide event.

That very afternoon, a stranger at school stopped me along the corridor. "Are you Wai Jia? Your classmate told me about you. I want to record your story during your launch. I'm a videographer. May I?"

On the day of the launch, hundreds of students from all around the world showed up. So large was the crowd that security guards locked the hall so we wouldn't break the fire code. God had orchestrated all this—more happened in those few weeks of prayer than in all the preceding months of my striving.

To date, the video of the launch continues to spread, impacting lives all around the world.[3]

Truly, prayer is the work. Prayer is the *greater* work.

Will you let God woo you into the secret place with Him? Will you allow Him to take over your calendar and rearrange your schedule? Not all of us can give up an entire Sunday for the Lord. You might be a mother of several young children with no help, or a healthcare worker who has to work weekends on a regular basis. But you can certainly set aside parts of your day to wrestle with God in prayer.

These are times best spent undisturbed in privacy, soaking in the sacredness of your time with the Lord. But they might also be minutes spent between serving customers or soaking in God's presence as you nurse a drowsy baby or even alone while mowing a lawn. Whatever it is, we're all called to spend time wrestling in prayer with Jesus. No one is absolved from this call.

Our dreams may seem too unimportant to take to God. We might think we shouldn't bother Him with them. But Hebrews 4:1 reminds us of the great need to enter into His rest "lest any of you seem to have come short of it." God knows how difficult it is to resist the demands of the world. Yet it's so simple. If we want to respond to Him with a big yes, we must be prepared to say no to the people and needs around us and take our dreams to Him.

The secret place is where we must all be. From the posture of rest and abiding, of desperate travail and wrestling in prayer, this is from where all our work and fruitfulness flow.

Contend for Your Breakthrough

In the days that followed, I vacillated between faith and doubt. An American lawyer wrote to me, saying she was committed to seeing Kitesong Global registered in the States. But it would cost five to eight thousand dollars. Where would I get the funds?

I began to pray.

The next morning a billowy snowstorm boxed everyone in. School and work were canceled throughout the city. The woods outside our home were blanketed a magical, mystical white. Yet of all days, an aged, wise American missionary friend we'd met in Singapore decided to drive seven hours from Pennsylvania just to spend the evening and next morning with us to catch up.

As I confided in him what was weighing on my heart, he said soberly, "If you could trust God to raise more than a hundred thousand dollars for the children's home in Nepal when you were eighteen years old, and that same amount to pay the tuition fees for you to come to Johns Hopkins—and to provide for your family—can you not trust Him for eight thousand? Can you not?"

I prayed again, deeper still. *God,* I said from a posture of humility, *I will not let you go until you bless me.*

The next morning, my phone rang. "Excuse me," I said to our missionary friend, then entered my bedroom. When I came out, I'm sure my face had washed white.

"What?" our guest asked.

"A mentor from Singapore called to catch up. He's offering a twenty-thousand-dollar check to help underwrite the costs of setting up Kitesong Global in the States."

I stood there, blinking, swaying slightly from shock.

Weeks later, Cliff drove us home from a friend's farmhouse. A glowing sun-orb was melting, and my heart was soaked heavy with prayer. *What is Kitesong Global? What is my life about? Who is Wai Jia?* But as the sky's aching beauty stilled my heart, it also swallowed up all my fears, and suddenly I wasn't afraid of that liminal space between dream-bearing and fulfillment.

Then as the world folded into a setting sun, I felt God whisper the meaning of the Chinese characters in my name, 蔚 (*Wei*) and 佳 (*Jia*). 蔚(*Wei*) represents the splendor and majesty of the skies, and 佳 (*Jia*)represents goodness and excellence. Then He said, *Your name encapsulates your life's and Kitesong Global's mission to reflect My splendor and goodness in the sky like a banner for all the world to see. That is what you were created for.*

That moment became a memorial stone. Months of prayer culminated in a God-encounter in a car, witness to God's eternal glory. Like Jacob, through wrestling in prayer, I received a new identity.

The months and years calloused with unanswered prayers reeled back with surprise at God's gift of breakthrough. It was worth it; it had all been worth it. Wrestling in prayer is always worth it.

Just because we don't understand the timing of God's promises doesn't give us the right to decide He must be mistaken. I learned that it is haughty—and precarious, even—to think that the dreams He's given us are not worth wrestling with Him in prayer. When we're befuddled by our own busyness, God may be provoked in love to put our hip out of joint. His invitation to rest and pray should be seized with gladness. Would you receive it?

If you've been overwhelmed by the grandeur of a dream God has given you and are tempted to get busy, don't. He is welcoming you to His throne room to wrestle with Him in prayer. He's not so religious that He can't take your unbridled questioning. He's not so pious that He can't handle your coarse doubts.

God brings us into the dark and keeps us there, waiting, not because He's cruel but because He *wants* us to wrestle, to search for the treasures that can only be gleaned in the throes of darkness. There is where He calls us into a deeper surrender, where He may choose to put a limp in us for the sake of a deeper dependence as we lean on Him.

So don't give up. In the darkness, when all seems lost, wrestle with God in prayer. And may you, like Jacob, be clothed with fresh revelation, deep transformation, and a new identity in God.

FOR REFLECTION

1. In your quest to obey God's call for your life, how have you ended up striving with your own strength?
2. What has resulted because of that striving? What kind of fruit has it borne?
3. What does "working from a posture of rest" mean and look like for you?

NEXT STEPS

1. Set aside some time to pray. Confess to God areas in your life where you've taken things into your own hands. Seek His forgiveness.
2. Ask God to show you how He wants you to rearrange your schedule to make time and space for deep prayer and intimacy with Him. Write down those new commitments.
3. What have you been wrestling with God about? Commit to praying through it until you receive your breakthrough.

PRAYER

God, you know I'm tempted to take things into my own hands. I've been so busy trying to make your dreams for me come to pass. I repent of my self-striving. Give me a revelation of the power of prayer. Give me the tenacity to wrestle with you in the secret place of prayer. Help me discover the wonder of your work when I surrender to you through a posture of rest. Let me, like Jacob, be clothed with a new identity as you do this deeper work in my life. Amen.

16

build your legacy of faith

> By faith Isaac blessed Jacob and Esau concerning things to come.
>
> —Hebrews 11:20

"Oh gosh," I said. I knew Cliff hadn't done it.

For months, our three-year-old, Esther-Praise, had been pleading with us to plant a shrubby lime tree in place of the sunflower that had died in our plot at the outdoor community garden downstairs from our apartment home in Singapore. Cliff and I discussed buying a lime graft and planting it, but with the overgrown weeds and soil hardened like rock, our will wavered. And with so many competing priorities as young parents, we just never got around to it.

Then as we walked home one day, we saw the most luscious, fruitful lime tree there ever was in our little plot of land. I stared at it in disbelief.

The kids ran to it, screaming, "Wow! God got it for us!"

"I so happy, I so happy!" Esther-Praise exclaimed, eyes wide open.

My mind raced for answers. Who had we told about our daughter's desire for a lime tree?

It must be Uncle Don, we decided. We took the elevator to the seventh floor to thank him, only to have him say, "I wish I could claim the credit, but it wasn't me."

That night, I stared out the window blankly, my heart pregnant with an aching longing. Who was it? No one knew.

Then I felt God tell me that in our insufficiencies and with our lack of time, energy, and expertise, He'd stepped in to fill the gap for Esther-Praise. He'd propelled someone we never told to take the trouble to buy a lime tree, uproot the weeds, soften the hard soil, and then plant our daughter's favorite tree. Both Sarah-Faith and Esther-Praise had realized this. "God got it for us!" they'd said.

Hebrews 11:20 says, "By faith Isaac blessed Jacob and Esau concerning things to come." Here, Isaac demonstrates faith in God, relying on Him to keep His word on His promises even when he couldn't see or understand everything. Isaac received the promises God gave to Abraham (Genesis 21:12) and then passed them along to his children. Even though he didn't know how they would come true, and amid significant family strife between his two sons and his wife (Genesis 27:1–40), Isaac exhibited faith and obeyed God even though he was elderly, nearly blind, and had not seen a total fulfillment of God's divine plan.

As I pondered this, it became clear to me that in the journey to obey God, there may be many instances when both parents and mentors come face-to-face with their shortcomings and inadequacies. There may be times when they wonder if they might have shortchanged their children's or others' blessings through their own weaknesses or even their choice to follow God.

I especially wondered about this with Cliff and me as parents. Perhaps Isaac had wondered where he'd gone wrong in his parenting when he discovered Jacob had stolen Esau's birthright and that their mother, Rebekah, had played a hand in it. Yet these setbacks didn't deter him from acting in faith and blessing his children. He passed on Abraham's blessing simply because He trusted God to bless His children and future generations, even despite his own limitations, beyond the end of his life.

In your journey to obey and follow God, do you wonder if you might have shortchanged your children or other loved ones by the sacrifices you've made? Do you long to believe that God will bless them deeply even when you may not see it in your lifetime? God calls us to deeper, greater trust. When we fail to bless our loved ones, He goes before and beyond us to bless them even beyond what we can see. All we need to do is trust and obey Him.

Cliff and I fell short of giving Esther-Praise her heart's desire, but I believe God saw her desire and provided the lushest, most fruitful lime tree—one far better than what her earthly father and I could provide.

If you're struggling with surrendering your children and your future generations to God, know this: He knows the end from the beginning. His promises never fail.

Like Isaac, will you trust that by building a legacy of faith because of your simple obedience to God's call you might assign to your children blessings in the future?

I hope my sharing a story of God's intimate provision for our children during a season of deep parental guilt will encourage you to obey God even when you cannot see what the future holds.

Trust God with Your Family

"She's going to miss that toy so much."

My voice soured with tears. While I knew Cliff and I had been called to a life of moving wherever and whenever God beckoned, it pricked my heart to know our children would be subject to a nomadic life. It was one thing to surrender ourselves to the cost of discipleship, but to subject our children to waiting on unknowns wrenched our hearts.

When we returned to Canada after my studies at Johns Hopkins were complete, we'd been gifted a comfortable home overlooking a forest. During that time, God blessed us with our second child and the extension of my no-pay leave so Cliff could serve as an executive pastor for a year. Canada's welfare system also meant Cliff's liver transplant issues were taken care of.

Now heading back to Singapore, where we had no home, meant the arduous task of resettling again. It meant Cliff would lose his insurance coverage in a land where medical bills are exorbitant. It meant saying goodbye to all the comforts we'd grown used to. Yet God reminded me to fulfill my integrity of completing the remaining year of my bond as a medical doctor in Singapore. We felt Him say, *By obeying Me, you are blessing your children in ways you cannot yet see.* Through tears, we said, "Yes, Lord."

But our packing process was pricked with grief. At Christmas, my mother-in-law had gifted Sarah-Faith a little toy ice-cream truck that fulfilled all the grand, eternal longings of a two-year-old. Cleverly designed, it had multicolored ice-cream flavors, animal cards that when inserted correctly sang out orders, and an electronic scoop that squealed out catchy choruses of delight. Sarah-Faith played with it every day. "My favorite, bestest toy ever!" she'd say.

Our move meant leaving behind what she loved most.

"Maybe we can take it with us?" Cliff suggested, almost serious, giving away his overindulgent fatherliness.

Our home in Canada was in the center of a cul-de-sac, and the news that we were leaving without knowing when we might return *and* without knowing where we would live in Singapore had been passed around like a parcel. A curiosity had joined the houses together, and I felt it closing in on me as questions asked with breathless anticipation found their way to me even when I tried to avoid them.

"What? You still don't know where you'll stay in Singapore? You don't have much time left!"

"How will you move homes with a three-month-old and a toddler?"

"How will you start work if you don't have accommodation in Singapore?"

My heart fluttered as I tried to field the questions, and I grew practiced at sweeping anxiety from my face. Still, I often found myself scrambling to swim back into shallow waters and counterfeit words, trying to sieve reassurance from my own thoughts to pass on to others.

The temporary accommodation options we'd found so far were either exorbitant or unsuitable. Then when a place within our budget finally came up, it was a one-bedroom apartment. For a family of four, with two little ones under three years of age—one a newborn—it would be a nightmarish adjustment.

One other fear I had concerned Sarah-Faith's eczema condition. Over the Canadian winter, her skin, once porcelain smooth, had erupted into a carpet of angry red discs all over her body. She scratched herself from neck to ankle. Even with moisturizing her skin five times a day and wrapping her with Vaseline under a wetsuit at night as a form of therapy, countless allergy tests, medication, and restriction diets, her condition worsened.

One afternoon a well-meaning neighbor strolled into our backyard and said to me, "Isn't Singapore extremely hot? Won't her skin get worse?"

With Esther-Praise swaddled and cradled in one of my arms and Sarah-Faith running around me, I struggled to hold back tears. It was our eleventh move in the past six years of marriage over four countries—Singapore, Uganda, the United States, and Canada. We had received our fair share of wagging fingers but more now that we had two children in tow.

"Have you thought about their futures?"

"Aren't you robbing them of a stable life?"

"Isn't it unhealthy to live this way?"

As time passed, my worries sprouted fronds that fingered their way into the future like tendrils. What about our daughters' sense of identity and heritage, let alone our housing, healthcare, insurance, and childcare needs?

In the quiet of the night, when everyone else was asleep, I found myself crying. With our other moves, Cliff and I had experienced God's provisions from taking leaps of faith. But this move felt different. With a toddler thick in her terrible twos, my postpartum self, and a defenseless newborn, I suddenly felt unable to take yet another leap. The how, what, and when questions became unanswerable. Even in my obedience, how was I being a blessing at all to my children?

Yet God continued to whisper, *Obey Me, and I will bless them.*

The weeks passed, and I began to press into God in prayer. He'd taught me that the legacy of a well-lived life is not in striving but in the pressing in with prayers of deeper clarity, greater definition. He was calling me to abandon the listless life of vague prayers and half-baked faith. He wanted me to enter into that sacred space of intercession, more so with family in tow, and in doing so discover the texture and tenacity, power and potency of well-defined, specific prayer.

Finally, an Australian volunteer from Kitesong Global shared that a family friend from Melbourne had a vacant three-bedroom apartment in Singapore. "Would you like to stay there for your first month in Singapore, until you find a suitable rental?"

As if God wanted to make it clear that this was divine providence and not merely coincidence, the homeowner's sister, who was staying in the apartment temporarily, planned to move out the very morning we would land in Singapore.

Now I sensed God whisper, *Does your family need anything I cannot provide?*

Where we fear to tread, God is already there.

Marvel at the Pursuit of God

Emboldened to deepen the specificity of my prayers, I confessed to Cliff, "I've been praying for a 'Singaporean Sarah' to love on Sarah-Faith as though she were like family to her."

He smiled knowingly. Sarah was a close American friend of ours, a homeschooling mom with three young sons who cared for a friend's little girl on a regular basis while her parents worked.

With our returning to Singapore, primarily for me to complete my work contract, I longed for a trusted mama friend to help Cliff—who would continue to be a stay-at-home parent—with caring for our exuberant toddler for a few hours each week while I was at work. Then he could work on his theological studies or get some respite. I wanted someone who would love Sarah-Faith like family and understand her serious eczema condition. So like a secret folded in origami, I hid the prayer in my heart.

A month before we left Canada, a lady I'd met only once years earlier reached out to me via text. I didn't know her well, but I knew she loved the Lord.

> *I know it will be hard for you all to adjust back to Singapore as a family. I homeschool my boys, and would very, very much like to take Sarah-Faith for homeschooling lessons, if you think it's a good idea. My husband and I prayed about it and are convicted not to charge you and Cliff for it because it's our ministry to you both. Sarah-Faith would be like family to us.*

Like family to us. Tears welled. The words *like family* were the very words I'd used in prayer.

I later found out that, like our friend Sarah, this lady had three little boys. The semblance was uncanny. When no one but Cliff knew my heart's desire, God did. In every sense, He provided our "Singaporean Sarah." Even when we couldn't see the future, He did. Just as how Isaac blessed his children as an act of faith, God taught me that He desires to see that kind of faith proclaimed over the future generations in our lives.

Easing me into our friendship, this lady regularly sent me photos of her children. *This is Daniel,* she wrote. *He has severe eczema. So don't worry, I know what to do with Sarah-Faith. She'll be comfortable in our home.*

I was scanning through more photos she sent me when my jaw froze. In the background of one of them was the exact toy ice-cream truck my mother-in-law had gifted Sarah-Faith!

Who bought that for your kids? I texted.

My mom bought it for my boys last Christmas.

What? No way! Cliff's mom bought it for Sarah-Faith last Christmas too!

I stared at the text, my mouth open with disbelief.

I felt God's gentle chiding. *Even with your best intentions, can anyone love your children more than I do?*

In Psalm 23:6, David says, "Surely goodness and mercy shall follow me all the days of my life." In Hebrew, the word for follow means "pursue." When we obey God, His beneficence seeks us out, for as a good Father, He is eagerly waiting to pour His love onto us. He is constantly working, constantly pursuing us, so He can bless us, generously and unbegrudgingly.

Days later, during a farewell visit, a close friend of Cliff's gave us a large set of Mega Bloks for our children. As soon as he gave it to us, my heart sank knowing there was no way we could take it to Singapore for them to enjoy. But two days later, a friend from Singapore who volunteered to help us collate kid items for our children before we landed texted with a photo, *I set aside this for you. Would you and your children like to have it?*

It was the exact same box of Mega Bloks as the one we had to leave behind. When no one else knew my heart's desires for our children's play and growth, God did. He provided an identical set of Mega Bloks, an identical toy ice-cream truck, as if asking me repeatedly, *Can you love your children more than I can? Have I ever left you or your family to sink when you obeyed Me to walk on water? Can you trust Me to bless your children in the future when you cannot yet see it?*

Filled with the assurance of His peace, the "moving must be so hard" comments suddenly seemed bizarre to me, because the joy of living constantly on the edge of God's gushing surprises made the petty suffering of uncertainty and packing insignificant.

In our pursuit to follow the dreams God has for us, He never requires hasty decisions that compromise our children's well-being. All He asks of us, as He did of Isaac, is to trust Him to bless our children "concerning things to come" (Hebrews 11:20).

After all, God knows the future. When we trust and obey, will our children not also be witnesses and recipients of a legacy of faith and obedience? I felt God tell me that, like Abraham, we must be willing to surrender our children to Him and trust Him to provide the ram in the thicket (Genesis 22:13–14). Isaac's life was a testimony of Abraham's faith. And through that inheritance of faith, he was able to pass on the blessings of faith to his children.

As we flew into Singapore, something in my spirit shifted. God had gone before us. And within the first two days of our landing, Sarah-Faith's skin, once red and angry, dissolved into a leathery texture that then became silky smooth again. My pediatrician colleague said in amazement, "Most kinds of eczema worsen horribly in the heat and humidity. Sarah-Faith's is the rare case that improves in it!" Our daughter's skin healed completely, and we never needed to seek treatment for eczema again.

As parents, it's natural for us to wonder if our stepping out in faith will be bad for our children. Surely in the physical, we would be safer, more secure, more stable. The less-radical life would certainly be more convenient. But what if the consequences of *not* walking in faith are graver because we exchange the spiritual foundations of our children—what could have grown to become a sea of faith—for sinking sand? What if our risk-taking in God might actually be good for them? I've felt God challenge me, *What if the questions you ask aren't whether this will jeopardize your children's stability or whether the risk is too great or what if they lose what they now have? What if instead you ask how their lives will be different? What your legacy of faith will be like for them?*

Deep down I knew God was smiling and saying, *When you obey Me, I will bless your children in ways you never expect.* God had gone into the future and pursued us with His goodness. These testimonies have become pages in journals of faith, belonging to both me *and* my children, for an eternal legacy.

If you fear taking risks, wishing to protect your children and other loved ones, I hope Hebrews 11:20 about Isaac's faith and these stories will remind you that we need not shield them from the God who blessed us with them. Just as how Isaac chose to in faith bless his children, may we likewise be encouraged to trust God and obey Him, and in doing so build up and hand down a rich legacy of faith for generations to come.

FOR REFLECTION

1. In your journey following God, what difficult decisions have you had to make concerning your children, mentees, grandchildren, or other loved ones?
2. How have some of these concerns affected you?
3. How has the knowledge that God's goodness will pursue you and these loved ones changed your perspective?

NEXT STEPS

1. Who are the loved ones you're most concerned about even as you take steps of faith to obey God? In a chart like this one, write their names in the first column.

Loved ones I'm most concerned about:	Specific prayer requests for each of them:	Marked as answered:

2. What specific prayer requests do you have for each of them? Write them in the second column.
3. Look forward to marking these prayer requests as answered in the third column.

PRAYER

God, I'm struggling with trusting you with my loved ones even as I take steps of faith to obey you. Yet I long for the faith of Abraham, who trusted you with his son. I long to trust you to bless my children as Isaac blessed his, even when his family circumstances were unfavorable. As I follow you into the unknown, will you grant me a deeper surrender as I put my loved ones into your hands? I know you love them more deeply than I can ever love them. Help me trust you in building my legacy of faith. Amen.

17

long for a better destination

> If they had been thinking of the country they had left, they would have had opportunity to return. Instead, they were longing for a better country—a heavenly one. Therefore God is not ashamed to be called their God, for he has prepared a city for them.
>
> —Hebrews 11:15–16 NIV

THIS WAS SO DISAPPOINTING. "Is there really no more room?"

"Take a look yourself, Wai Jia."

I looked at the U-Haul truck, filled to the brim for our move from Canada to the States but with no stroller or crib. We'd packed only the bare minimum for our five-month-old, taking one grocery bag of baby clothes. I thought, *What kind of mom am I? With all the poop and spit, we'll go through these clothes in just three days!*

But we accepted this as part of our journey following God's call, and "Travel light" was our motto.

A day and a half of driving later, we finally reached our townhouse estate in Baltimore. As we drove into the entrance, a large stocky man wearing a white singlet ambled toward us, arms stretched out to greet us. Who was he? A contractor, plumber, or resident manager?

"Hi, I'm Sam. I live across from you. You look like you could use a hand."

When we walked into the apartment, we found a stroller, a high chair, and dozens of other baby items we would need. An alumni had moved out and left them there. My heart swelled.

The next day, Sam returned holding a bulging trash bag over his shoulder. "My daughter has outgrown these," he said. In the bag I found a pile of clothes for a child six to nine months old, just what Sarah-Faith would need in the coming months.

God knew, and He'd gone before us.

Hebrews 11:16 says, "Truly if they had called to mind that country from which they had come out, they would have had opportunity to return. But now they desire a better, that is, a heavenly country. Therefore God is not ashamed to be called their God, for He has prepared a city for them." Unlike the Israelites who complained and desired to return to Egypt, the patriarchs of faith such as Abraham, Isaac, and Jacob continued to trust God for His promises of inheriting the promised land even though they were not fulfilled in their earthly lifetimes. They were willing to endure hardship and the discomforts of sojourning into a foreign land without any citizenship rights because they understood that God's ultimate destination for them was a heavenly city (Hebrews 11:10).

If they were looking for earthly comforts, they could have returned to their homelands. Yet they did not, counting themselves as "strangers and pilgrims on the earth" (Hebrews 11:13). The concluding word *therefore* in Hebrews 11:16 tells us how their faith and obedience pleased God.

In the same way, God desires for us to press onward and upward with our eyes fixed on eternity rather than to look back on where we were before. When and if God calls us to move outside our comfort zones, will we be willing? If and when He calls us out of our spheres of influence to enter new, unfamiliar territories, will we say yes? Only being captivated by an eternal perspective of a better dwelling place (Revelation 21:9–14) and trusting that God has gone before us to prepare the way will help us endure our earthly uncertainties.

I hope my story of God's miraculous provision through another cross-continental move, this time with a toddler and newborn, will encourage you to trust Him. Would you dare to risk following God even if it means never looking back? May your desire for a better "heavenly country" and trust in His going before you enable you to find instances of God's tender care amid life's harrowing transitions and encourage you to face your uncertainties with courage.

Look to a Better Home

During our move to Singapore from Canada, several things were misplaced, one of which was Sarah-Faith's first, one and only backpack.

It was a little blue owl backpack, a gift from a lady at church in Canada. I teared receiving it as even before we had children, I'd seen the exact same one at a store in Singapore and thought, *Oh, this would be cute if we had kids.*

Then we lost it during our move.

"Mama," Sarah-Faith, then two years of age, would say, "I want owl backpack!"

Sheepishly, I would tell her, "Mama is still looking for it." But deep down, I knew it was gone forever.

In the initial weeks back in Singapore, an acute loneliness hit me hard. Even though I was in my home country again, the reverse cross-cultural shock and adjustments to mothering two young children disoriented me. I felt like a stranger in my own city.

One afternoon, with my daughters in tow, I visited our "Singaporean Sarah" homeschooling-mom friend in her far-away housing estate, hoping to get to know her family better. When I first arrived, I felt tense. Somehow, the apartments felt too crowded and too high, and the weather seemed too hot. Amid the concrete jungle of Singapore, I gasped for respite from the humidity, longing for the cool breeze blowing from the forest behind our home in Canada.

"Why did we have to come back?" I muttered rhetorically. "Canada had become so much more comfortable to live in." Like the Israelites reminiscing about their times in Egypt, I began to murmur.

As I lingered at the nearby playground, a voice startled me. "Are you Wai Jia?" I nodded, and this stranger said, "Someone shared your testimony with me through Facebook some time ago. I know this sounds weird, but I feel God wants me to link you up with mothers near you so we can support you and your family in your transition back home."

I could have hugged her. All week I'd been praying, *God, will you help me find community again?*

Shortly after, I was connected to a few new moms. *I will be your pit stop for any baby items you need,* texted one. I barely knew her. Days later, I drafted a response to her, then deleted it, then redrafted it. For days I looked at the text, afraid to send it. *I hate imposing. She'll think I'm a bother.*

Several weeks later, I finally plucked up the courage to ask if she might have a toddler's backpack to pass down. Attaching a photo to the text, I confessed shyly, *I lost Sarah-Faith's favorite owl backpack. Here's how it looks. Happy to have any backpack as long as it doesn't have Disney princesses plastered all over it.*

I decided to try to convince my two-year-old that a different backpack, however it looked, was better than the one we lost. But the reply I got shocked me. A photo of the exact same blue owl backpack stared back at me.

This was passed down to me a while ago. I was supposed to pass it on to my helper when she returned to Philippines a few months ago, but my daughter hid this backpack in her own room, and so it's still with me. It's yours.

Tears streamed down my cheeks, and the love of God overwhelmed me like a hug.

So often we think we have to experience some grand encounter with a spiritual being to understand who God is. But more often, in the little things is where He makes Himself known to us, not only as Creator but as Father.

I thought about the chain of events that led to this moment—the loss of the backpack from Canada, the serendipitous meeting with a stranger in a new neighborhood far away from where we were staying, the connection to this particular mom, my fear and reluctance to reach out, the gifting to the Filipino helper that didn't work out—and marveled at the tenuous sequence of those events that culminated in this divinely orchestrated moment for God to write *Love* large on our hearts.

There were many instances I wanted to fly back to Canada. Back there, we had everything we needed. Yet in that moment I realized how trust in God for a "better destination" and our resulting obedience makes room for His provision and miracles. I had a glimpse of how His going before us to prepare what we needed symbolized His heart of preparing an eternal, heavenly dwelling place that far exceeds our expectations.

The question for ourselves is this: Will we trust Him enough to progress onward toward new destinations He calls us to? Or will we shirk back to live within our comfort zones?

As my two-year-old proudly posed in a hand-me-down shirt and shoes and showed off her backpack, I caught a glimpse of her childlike gratitude. While all I saw was a well-used backpack fraying at the edges, a shirt with stains and shoes that were well-worn, all Sarah-Faith saw was a collection of perfect gifts. "Mama, look at my new shirt—cats with glasses! I love my backpack!" She beamed.

Like Abraham, Isaac, and Jacob, Sarah-Faith had seen beyond earthly possessions to appreciate what God had done. He'd gone before her to provide what she needed. It blows my mind that He, the Creator of the universe, had already planned this even before our family had taken the step of faith to move back to Singapore.

Can we bring this childlike faith on our faith journeys? We may not have the same material comforts as we did back in our homelands, but as we press on in faith, can we carry that childlike expectation and eager anticipation of God's faithfulness to prepare a better, heavenly country for us? Can we trust that He has prepared a city for us?

Through the incident of the little blue owl backpack, I heard God's sacred echoes resounding through the quiet. I saw His grace interlaced through all our tiring moves and heard Him tell us that our move back to Singapore was intentional, directly in the center of His will.

If you feel overwhelmed or stressed by the provisions your family needs by following God's will, know this: He knows what you all need far more than you do. All the resources in heaven and on earth belong to Him (Psalm 50:10–12). Most of all, He wants to invite you into a place He's already prepared for you, even when you can't imagine it.

Like Abraham, we must walk out our faith with God on a day-to-day basis, preparing ourselves for the day He might call us to give up what we most treasure. When our only choice is to trust, we must believe that as we say goodbye to the things and places so dear to our hearts, God will provide hope through a better destination.

How different things would have looked had the Israelites pressed forward in earnest expectation instead of complaining that they missed the food they'd had in Egypt while they were still slaves! (Exodus 16:1–3; Numbers 11:4-6). God is calling our spirits into deeper trust and greater freedom in Him.

I admit, it would have been far easier for us to stay in Canada, in quiet suburbia, with our green backyard overlooking a quiet forest in uneventful serenity. It would have saved us the cost of long flights, the inconvenience of packing, the anxiety of possibly having no place to stay when we landed, the stresses of constantly moving. And what about the uncertainty of perhaps again moving to a developing country we felt God leading us to—as we did with Uganda—entering yet another unknown future in a rural place with questionable security, healthcare, and education?

Yet few of us consider the dangers of staying safe. Too few of us understand the perils of living our lives in comfort and luxury when we fail to realize how much we deprive ourselves—and our children—of the many miracles, great and small, God orchestrates on our behalf when we let go of what means so much to us. Too few of us understand the gravity of robbing ourselves of the opportunity to witness the reality of God when we hold back out of fear.

If today you're holding back out of fear of what might happen to you and your family, remember God is already on the other side. He's prepared a heavenly city, a better dwelling place. For everything you've surrendered or left behind or given up, even if it's your beloved home and everything you've ever known, know that He loves you and your family far too much to leave you to sink. When you obey Him to walk on water, there He will be to receive you on the other side.

FOR REFLECTION

1. If God has called you to a new season, how has it been difficult to let go of your previous one and prepare to embrace what He's called you to?

2. What will you grieve the most when you leave your current station?
3. What are you looking forward to in the next season? Share specific prayer requests in confidence to God.

NEXT STEPS

1. Recall or write down your testimony about how God met you before when you walked in faith toward a new destination.
2. As you place your trust in God, what do you sense Him speaking to you about your next destination? Write down these revelations.
3. Take some time to ask the Lord to show you a picture of your heavenly dwelling place. Write down or draw what He shows you.

PRAYER

God, thank you for calling me out of my comfort zone. Today I commit to desiring a better destination in my future, trusting that you have prepared a better, heavenly dwelling place for me. I confess that I'm afraid of the unknown, yet I know you're already there waiting for me. I choose to walk forward in faith today and marvel at the future and eternal rewards you already have laid out for me and my household. Amen!

18

embrace small beginnings

> Therefore from one man, and him as good as dead, were born as many as the stars of the sky in multitude—innumerable as the sand which is by the seashore.
>
> —Hebrews 11:12

I LAY IN BED ONE NIGHT, my heart heavy. An apocryphal sense of dread had landed on my chest after the COVID-19 lockdown measures were announced.

"I never thought we'd live through a time like this," I told my husband.

"Me neither." He sighed.

Rolling over to face him, I whispered, "Do you think they'll call doctors like me back to help?"

"They could." He shrugged. "It's getting pretty bad."

By then, COVID-19 had ravaged through dozens of high-density dormitories, infecting tens of thousands of migrant workers. Public hospitals were mass-deploying healthcare workers to these buildings, and an unprecedented disaster was unfolding before our very eyes.

I sat up, straight as a rod, my voice stricken with fear. "Take that back, Cliff. Say they won't. I won't know how to help. I can't."

I'd been out of clinical work for seven years. I conducted research, taught medical students, and pursued public health, but I no longer felt confident seeing patients. Memories, long suppressed, came flooding back.

"You stupid, stupid house officer!" the senior doctor at the emergency department yelled. A house officer is a new medical graduate in a clinical apprenticeship, and as he hurled vulgarities at me, I wanted to disappear. Another time, I held a patient's hand to reassure her that she would be discharged soon, only to find her dead from a massive heart attack the next morning. My seniors assured me it was an unforeseen event, but the incident stained me forever. I never quite recovered.

Gradually, I inched away from clinical work and found comfort in the realms of public health and medical education. Then when COVID-19 broke out, I was asked to teach medical students since they were barred from the wards. Yet my mind drifted—*I really should be helping at the frontlines*.

One day I suffered a health complication requiring urgent surgery, and I was bed-bound for a week. As I recovered in the luxury of my own home, I watched the world outside spin out of control. The pain of seeing a pandemic play out while I did nothing became unbearable.

But how would I even begin to help? I thought. *Cliff is immunocompromised because of his liver transplant. My two children are less than three years of age, and I'm still nursing. Are my clinical skills still of any use at all? Would I only be a burden?*

I thought of the many months my supervisor, director of the emergency department, had sat with me at the Jewel Café near our offices at the university week after week, mentoring me. Through his kind leadership, he rehabilitated my confidence. While I'd been verbally abused at the emergency department at another hospital more than a decade ago, it felt like no coincidence that God chose the director of this emergency department to nurture me back to vocational health.

But now in the furrows of an unfolding national disaster, I found myself weeping, pleading to God for answers. For all my accolades related to public health, I felt useless in this national crisis.

Huddled near our balcony one evening, I cried to Cliff, "How can this be, that after God sent me all the way to Johns Hopkins to birth Kitesong Global to help the world, I now stand here in the throes of a pandemic with nothing to offer?"

I was afraid of this new feeling inside me. Something was awakening, something dead and ossified was breathing into life, and I was petrified.

When God stirs your heart with His dreams and promises, do you tremble? Hebrews 11:12 says, "Therefore from one man, and him as good as dead, were born as many as the stars of the sky in multitude—innumerable as the sand which is by the seashore." When God spoke to Abraham about His promise, Abraham was an old man, considered "as good as dead" by the world. I wonder if he received God's promises with fear and trembling.

Yet Hebrews 11:12 shows us the implications of Abraham and Sarah's faith—that even if it was imperfect, it resulted in the birth of a multitude of people, as many as the stars of the sky.

I hope my next story of imperfect faith through my own fumbling journey will encourage you not to despise your little faith and small beginnings but to trust God for His final outcome.

God Embraces Our Meager Offerings

As I cried to God to use me, my prayer became more audacious: *God, bring me to the dormitories to help the migrant workers.*

"It's impossible to gain access," I was told. "They're locked down."

Then, a miracle. I called my supervisor, now suddenly placed in charge of COVID-19 isolation facilities for migrant workers.

"I want to help," I told him. "I don't know how. I probably don't remember how to see patients anymore. But I want to help."

"Then come," he said. "Come back to the frontlines with me. If you trust me, I will help you."

The next morning a nonprofit migrant worker organization reached out to me. "Can you help us access the largest dormitory in Singapore housing twenty-five thousand workers?"

That same afternoon my supervisor asked me if I knew of any nonprofit organizations that could help with migrant workers' welfare. There I was, at the uncanny convergence of both their requests. I knew God was at work.

"Let me connect you," I replied. "Let's meet at the dormitory."

The next day, on Good Friday, I was in a state of shock at my promptly answered prayer. There we all were at a sprawling, fully-locked-down dormitory in Singapore. I'd gone in my casual clothes, thinking we were in for a quick, look-see reconnaissance trip.

But no. My eyes widened as hundreds of medical workers in full-blown PPE (personal protective equipment) marched toward me, setting up medical tents and stations with immaculate precision. Distinguished professors in collared shirts huddled in a corner together, murmuring in low tones.

I felt all eyes on me, this foreign body in lavender exercise clothes who did not belong among this faultless army of soldiers. A medical officer threw a set of scrubs at me, his eyes glowering with irritation at my breaking an unspoken code.

At once, my mind went blank. I didn't know where to stand, what to do. As if fully aware of the internal travail within me, my supervisor smiled benevolently and passed me a mask, gown, and goggles.

"Here's your stethoscope too. Let's start seeing patients."

I stared at him, incredulous. "Me?"

"You and I are the only doctors at this station."

A kind nurse helped me as I fumbled with the PPE. "No, not like that. Like this," she said.

I slipped on my gloves, but touched a table.

"Aw shucks, now you gotta change 'em, Doctor."

I degloved, then re-gloved clumsily.

Under the heat of the protective gown, I felt faint, and above the nearly suffocating N95 mask, my goggles misted. Yet I felt God's cool, refreshing touch as He whispered, *I've answered your prayer—to be useful. And better still, at the frontlines.*

After nearly a decade away from clinical work, here I was seeing patients again. "Brother, do you have cough? Fever? Runny nose?" I looked into the eyes of the migrant workers, filled with fear, and despite language barriers tried to build a bridge of understanding to reassure them it would be all right.

On the way home I wept, shaking.

Leaving my shoes outside our apartment and then skirting through the door sideways so I wouldn't touch anything, I asked Cliff to bring me a change of clothes and bleach in a bucket to disinfect my scrubs. I didn't want to risk passing on the virus to him or our children.

As I washed my hair with tears streaming down, I remembered Jesus' death on the cross and what it represents—total surrender. I remembered what God requires is not capability but availability, surrender, and obedience. While the world champions vessels of might and power, God looks for broken ones, eager to be refashioned for fitful use in the Master's hands. And like the widow with two mites, there I was with my meager offering of faded clinical skills, shaky confidence, and a clinical trauma complex.

But God did not despise the widow. Instead, He loved and embraced her offering. And even though Sarah and Abraham were an elderly couple with imperfect faith, God used their faith in mighty ways, blessing them with a vast inheritance and legacy. That Good Friday, as I pondered how Jesus' death was His seeming weakness that ushered in history's greatest victory, God smashed my self-doubts.

My supervisor texted me that night. *You still have much to offer, Wai Jia.* I knew God was calling me to embrace my meager offering, to place my two mites, my five loaves and two fish, in His hands.

God Calls Us to Be Faithful Even If We're Broken

Within a few days, great acceleration took place. I took on retraining and deployment opportunities. At the frontlines, God opened my eyes firsthand to the problems on-ground—not only the language barriers between medical personnel and migrant workers but a rising, restless anxiety among the workers amid rapidly changing rules and regulations.

Soon my supervisor called me and asked, "Can you illustrate a health booklet for the isolation facilities and translate them? We have thousands of workers here, and they have no idea what's going on. Can you help?"

Instead of gratitude at being asked to help address a problem I'd seen with my own eyes, I felt a rising indignation. *For all my public health accolades, is this what I've been reduced to now—a cartoonist?*

As if he'd read my thoughts, Cliff promptly said to me, "This morning's devotional from Oswald Chambers is for you. It's from Ecclesiastes 9:10. 'Whatever your hand finds to do, do it with your might.'"

I glowered at him in mock irritation. "Why do you always know what I'm thinking?"

Day and night, I worked on the health booklet, and suddenly all the skills and gifts inside of me came alive. The fact that I was swabbing workers at the frontlines gave me access to the tangible problems in health communication on-ground, and I soon realized that the infrastructure and expertise Kitesong Global had in content creation, volunteer recruitment, and translation were perfect for filling the communication gaps in the outbreak. All the networks I'd accumulated in the nonprofit sector over the years became immensely useful, assisting us with real-time feedback and pooling resources.

One afternoon I received an email from the chairperson of the steering committee of the World Health Organization Global Outbreak Alert Response Network (GOARN) of Singapore. *We need to talk.*

Who? Me? Surely he was mistaken.

"You are exactly who we need in this outbreak," he said. "Do you see this?" He showed me a huge web of diagrams. "This is Risk Communication and Community Engagement—RCCE. That's the huge gap you're filling right here in our outbreak response. Now seriously, where did you come from? You just popped up out of nowhere!"

Before I knew it, he was mentoring me, honing my skills for this important pillar of outbreak response that had been sorely neglected. The booklets became posters, the posters became face-to-face engagements and workshops, and then these snowballed into a multimodal nationwide movement to empower marginalized communities.

I found myself training others to conduct facilitated Kitesong Global workshops with quarantined migrant workers, using our books and animations translated into Bengali, Tamil, and Mandarin to convey key health messages. Workers penned their dreams on kites they made, pinning them up all around the sterile isolation facilities, sharing with one another the hopes they had for when the outbreak was over.

One migrant worker shared his kite with me. I looked at him, blinking back tears as I held it, a powerful symbol of freedom yet made of barricade tape, a symbol of imprisonment. He told me, "I draw my daughter on kite. My dream is she become doctor like you, go help other people. That is my dream."

At once it became clear to me that God had created Kitesong Global and me for such a time as this. Doors had flung open. What started as an organic initiative bloomed into a nationwide movement involving regional health clusters, government authorities, and migrant worker NGOs (non-governmental organizations). The Geneva headquarters of the World Health Organization invited me as a keynote speaker to talk about this nationwide RCCE movement, offering nearly two hundred thousand dollars to fund our growing initiative.

I held back tears as I mulled over how differently God looks at our offerings. Though the world saw as an old man when they looked at Abraham—"as good as dead"—he was exactly who God wanted to use to fill the earth with his descendants. In the same way, God doesn't despise our two mites nor our five loaves and two fish. However useless we may feel about ourselves, however ashamed we may feel about what little we have to offer, God cherishes that we might have "put in more than all" the others when we give it with all our hearts (Luke 21:3).

Because I said yes to that still, small voice in my heart, God used me. He made a vessel that was so broken and so useless in the eyes of the world to bear fruit. I had goose bumps, thinking that at eighteen years of age I had written on my medical application with innocent naivete, "My hope is that someday I can partner with the United Nations and World Health Organization meaningfully to make an impact on our world."

God fulfilled that dream, not through my own striving seeking opportunities, but simply by my being obedient when He asked for a simple yes to drawing cartoons. He showed me the beauty of embracing small beginnings instead of despising them. (In the last chapter of this book, I'll share more of how God brought this dream to fulfillment to an even greater extent.)

I learned that when God calls us to say yes, He wants us to embrace doing so with delight even if those beginnings seem small or unglamorous. We can be sure that God is there already, simply inviting us to experience the joy of service with Him as He fronts the battle for us. All He requires of us is a little bit of faith and trust in His promises.

Weeks later, as I walked into my office, a distant mentor unaware of all that was unfolding in my life left a gift for me. I opened the bag to find a book titled *A Jewel in His Crown* by Priscilla Shirer. At once the Holy Spirit came over me. Overwhelmed with emotion, I saw a vision of the Jewel Café, where my supervisor had spent week after week mentoring me. I closed my eyes and saw the Lord Himself placing a jewel in my crown. Then I sensed Him say, *For all the years you felt broken and useless, I used those mentoring talks at the Jewel Café to restore the jewel in your crown.*

Despite my low self-confidence, God Himself rehabilitated me into the leader I was meant to be. And at the height of the outbreak when my confidence blossomed, the Jewel Café stopped its operations temporarily, as if telling me His work to restore my crown had been done.

Do you face seemingly unsurmountable internal challenges like past trauma complexes, abusive experiences, or ungodly beliefs that hold you back from being who you're meant to be? Remember Hebrews 11:12, which tells us that even when the world considered Abraham "as good as dead," God chose him to bear descendants, as many as the sand on the seashore. What the world deems nothing more than a small beginning can grow to so much more in God's hands.

Your faith may be small, your confidence shaky. But who knew that my fumbling faith would end up helping tens of thousands of COVID-19–positive, marginalized migrant workers during the global pandemic and propel me to fulfilling my dream of partnering the World Health Organization? It started with embracing a small beginning, simply by saying yes to God.

Like the widow, would you give God your two copper coins? Like the little boy with his lunch, would you give Him your five loaves and two fish?

Never despise your little faith of small beginnings, for only God knows the amazing fruit it might bear in years to come.

FOR REFLECTION

1. What has been the hardest part about your small beginnings?
2. What setbacks or abuses hinder your self-confidence?
3. What do you think you have to offer to God?

NEXT STEPS

1. In a symbolic gesture, place your weaknesses and past hurts at the Lord's feet. Ask Him to use them for His glory.
2. List your strengths, however imperfect they might be. Tell God these are your genuine offerings to Him.
3. Close your eyes and come into a time of intimacy with God. Despite the setbacks and abuse you might be facing, what does He say about who you really are and your abilities? Write down these precious revelations.

PRAYER

God, I long to do more for your glory even as I struggle to overcome what holds me back. Yet I know you see me differently. You adore the contrite and brokenhearted, and you give strength to the lowly. Will you renew my spirit and help me put my little faith in your hands? You can turn water into wine, five loaves and two fish into a magnificent miracle. Help me embrace my small beginnings. Will you use me, as you did Abraham and Sarah in their weaknesses, to fulfill your greatest purposes? Amen.

19

rest in God

> He waited for the city which has foundations, whose builder and maker is God.
>
> —Hebrews 11:10

THE CONFIRMATION that we were being ousted from our rented home brought me to my knees. The children had been playing nearby, and I steadied myself on a kitchen stool while molding my anguish into a forced smile as they came to give me a hug.

Yes, our lease agreement was ending soon, and we'd planned to transition back to the mission field, wherever God might call us. But with the closing of travel doors due to COVID-19 and my growing involvement in migrant worker engagement with the World Health Organization, we felt the Lord's leading to instead stay another year in Singapore.

Cliff had asked the landlord to extend our lease, and then we'd looked around knowing he might not agree to our request. But we still hoped for the best as we awaited his response. One night I dreamed we were viewing another home, and when I woke up, a sense of dread filled my chest. True enough, the next day our landlord replied coldly, "I want to sell the unit. I won't extend your lease. You have only a few weeks to move."

Overwhelmed by that familiar feeling of not knowing where our next home would be, I felt weighed down by the sandstone of responsibility. Once again, I wondered if we were selfish—foolhardy, even—to think we could lead the nomadic pilgrim's life, living lightly to be ready to say *Yes, Lord, here we are* at the drop of a hat. Especially as the parents of two little girls.

The unknown felt so . . . uncertain. Yet from experience, we knew that uncertainty is the foundation for faith to come to full fruition. While the answer of rejection was painful, part of us knew it was the start of God's beginning a new chapter of faith for us. Nonetheless, that night I asked the Lord, *What now?*

What an ironic situation, I thought. We had a perfectly good home in Canada, but here we were called to stay in Singapore at the mercy of a landlord eager for us to move out. I thought about the homes we'd left behind and all the heartache, stress, and trauma that followed our dozen moves across four countries in ten years.

I admit that following God is not always easy, rational, or safe. Yet it is right and ultimately worth it. If He'd done it before, if He'd provided a home for us every time we needed one, He'd do it again. I could look toward a better future where faith already dwelled.

Abraham, too, suffered the pains of sojourning. Yet he was able and willing to dwell in tents in the land of promise as a pilgrim because he had eternity in mind. He "waited for the city which has foundations, whose builder and maker is God" (Hebrews 11:10). In Greek, this implies he was expecting an eternal dwelling place with eager anticipation (Romans 8:19).[1] Despite suffering many transitions, what kept Abraham grounded was his faith in "receiving a kingdom which cannot be shaken" (Hebrews 12:28; see also 13:14).

Revelation 21:2–14 gives us a glimpse of New Jerusalem, a feature of God's eventual conquest over sin and death, revealing to us how the patriarchs' faith propelled them to believe that God's ultimate purpose for their lives was not measured by earthly means but by heavenly ones.[2]

Similarly, the journey of faith requires us to wait on God to enter fully into His promises, and this waiting often requires a slowing down and entering into the fullness of His rest (Hebrews 4:1).

I hope my next story, about how God revealed to me the importance of a Sabbath heart and a posture of waiting, will encourage you to wait on God, to enter into that restful space of communion with Him, and to look toward your heavenly home as the ultimate inheritance and prize.

Enter into His Rest

One morning I felt God inviting me to spend time with Him on the beach. So clear was His invitation, and yet my heart resisted. I had the great urge to instead scour for home rental listings. I couldn't sit back and do nothing, could I?

Yet His voice beckoned, *Come away with Me.*

At the beach, my skin soaked up His Spirit like a parched ground does water. I was spent, dry inside. I'd experienced four rounds of burnout from battling the COVID-19 crisis at the frontlines, and that's when our landlord had given us the notice to leave. Because of the outbreak and how often I'd been activated, I worked through several weekends without rest. Joy leaked away from me as I trundled on. We'd had to cancel our plans to visit Cliff's family in Canada, and now the burden of our empty home there, crumbling and costing us a large sum in tax payments, weighed heavy on us. And for weeks, looking for a new home in Singapore had come to no avail.

I lay on the sand, overtaken by God's presence. In desperation I silently cried, *I give up, Lord. Will you choose a home for us? Surely your choice will be better than ours*. But instead of His revealing a vision of a home or address, I sensed Him tell me, *Choose to rest and wait on Me.*

I looked at the sea, a perfect bowl reflecting the sky, and experienced a startling revelation. God is continually creating masterpieces in sunsets and sunrises. Like ours, His work is never fully finished. There's always more to do. Yet if even the God of the universe took a day to rest and called it holy, how could I not?

Suddenly, I discovered a reorientation, a fresh perspective that allowed God to come through. My waiting on and resting in Him was giving way to new possibilities. Prayer was steadying my heart to surrender to the weight of the revelation when it came. It dawned on me that choosing to leave practical things undone, toys unkept, and work unfinished to rest and wait on God is a grand, heroic act of trust.

Like Abraham, who waited on the heavenly city with eager expectation rather than anxiously striving, we must trust that God, our all sufficiency, is enough to complete what our ordinary human efforts cannot. Rest acknowledges our frailties, foibles, and failings. Waiting invites Christ to come into our lives to commune with us even when the vision has yet to be fulfilled.

There on the beach, I said aloud, "Lord, here I am," relinquishing my desire to be in control, my need for a home. I simply said yes to prioritizing rest and waiting on Him. In Exodus 16:22–24, we learn how God told the people to gather twice as much bread before Sabbath and then set aside Sabbath as a day holy unto the Lord. This was the only instance where the manna didn't stink or grow worms the next day, reminding us that as we trust God with Sabbath, our obedience begets His provisions. He is faithful to provide what we need.

I repented for having little faith. And as soon as surrender arrived a bizarre question came: *What more about the dream?* God whispered.

What more? In that dream I'd had, our housing agent showed us a beautiful but cramped apartment boasting extravagant facilities that cost more than three million dollars. It was unaffordable. And too small. Somewhere we'd never be happy.

Suddenly, my eyes widened. What seemed like an unintentional meander in casual conversation with God was in fact completely purposeful. God had spoken, and I gasped aloud at the invisible made visible. In the hot noonday sun, goose bumps prickled all over me like a cold shiver.

Our housing agent was the wrong one!

I was sure the Lord was smiling at me. I'd waited on Him in the quiet space of rest and found Him waiting there for me all along.

So which agent is right? I asked. God downloaded what I needed to know in a heartbeat, and I immediately contacted my father's housing agent.

Wait on God with Expectancy

The next day, the agent—a wide, stocky man with thick-rimmed glasses and an unshaven face—showed up at our doorstep. "So tell me," he said, "of all the homes you've stayed in, which is your favorite?"

Nervously but nostalgically, I said, "Most of all, I loved the old, spacious bungalow we house-sat when we returned from Uganda, because it was next to the nature reserve filled with monkeys and wildlife, and it was so peaceful. I didn't care that it was old; it was beautiful."

His eyes lit up. "Do you know how many homes I've searched out for you over the past few months? But I finally shortlisted one as my top choice, and it's exactly in that neighborhood! I just know you will love it."

I looked at him, puzzled. How did he know we needed to look for a home even before we did? Then to my shock, I discovered that he was the same man who fourteen years earlier had worked for my father and connected him with that returning Singaporean missionary from Nepal. He'd even urged him to let me take that trip!

Now I was standing before the human vessel God had used to begin a chain of events that would change my life through *Kitesong*, then used him again through his switching careers to become a housing agent. God had used a dream He gave me followed by a specific word to lead me right back to this man.

"Okay, we don't delay. No home to stay in is no fun. Next week you follow me la." He spoke in rich, local vernacular with an excited flourish.

But when I googled the apartment, to my horror I discovered it was in a forty-four-year-old building. By Singaporean standards, that's exceedingly old for a residential place. I kept my expectations low. And on the day of viewing, from afar I could see peeling paint, broken tiling, and thick carpets of moss growing on the sides of the building.

We got into the elevator. "Which floor?" I asked the agent. "I sure miss staying on the top floor like I did as a child in my first home!"

He smiled a toothy grin. "Your favorite floor loh—all the way to the top! Twenty-first floor leh!"

The elevator door opened, and I nearly staggered. There, beyond the apartment's windows, lay everything I'd dreamed for in a home—a forest, a lake, a melting sunset. So high up were we that we could see above the tall palm trees swaying like reeds in the wind. Rain-forest tree branches and vines entwined, peeking through the low clouds that hung over them like a magical mist. Instantly, we were transported into another world. A pair of yellow orioles flew by. A chorus of crickets and birdsong rang loudly in the distance.

"You like it?" the agent asked, almost bouncing, beaming with pride at his good taste.

"Yes, I like it." But I knew an apartment this old would be riddled with problems. I imagined us saddled with all sorts of issues to fix. Besides, we couldn't afford to buy a home of this size—and I told him so.

"That's all I need to know." A furrow appeared between the agent's brows. "Okay, then. You just pray. Leave the rest to me, okay."

We agreed to a housing inspection, and after it took place, Cliff revealed to me, "The inspectors told me to wait for two hours because they expected lots of issues for a home this old. But they found only minor issues, and they were done quick."

But we still couldn't afford it.

Days after that, the housing agent told us, "I found someone who will buy this home for you to live in as long as you're in Singapore. No questions asked. It's a done deal. It's yours!"

What? I marveled at what God had done. This miracle happened not through my striving but by my entering rest with God.

Luke 18:29–30 became real to me. Jesus said to the disciples, "There is no one who has left house or parents or brothers or wife or children, for the sake of the kingdom of God, who shall not receive many times more in this present time, and in the age to come eternal life."

I closed my eyes, and tears welled behind my eyelids. God was and is always faithful. How divine that He revealed His dream home for us only when I finally let go of returning to Canada, when I finally let go of the idea of begging our Singaporean landlord to extend our lease, when I finally decided to make God's home within me and to set up Sabbath as a tabernacle in my heart.

God spoke to me then, asking me to always wait on Him with great expectancy for things He would do in the future, in the same way the patriarchs of faith looked to Him for their eternal dwelling.

Will you trust God by "wasting time" and sitting at His feet? Faith in God to provide for our needs in the future is a brave commitment to His ability. Yet our faith in His ability *despite* our rest is a deeper, braver surrender.[3] It says, *God, you are greater than I.* Sabbath is His gift of love to us. If you're feeling spent and weary, overwhelmed by your future's uncertainty, it could be the perfect reminder of how desperately you need to rest and simply wait in expectancy for God's revelations to unfold.

Perhaps what more of us need is not more striving or working toward our dreams but an intentional sowing into the extravagant wastefulness of time, in unapologetic playfulness, in indulgent communion with Jesus.[4] That could be the most fruitful, faith-filled act we choose in our lives. As Abraham looked to the future with lenses of eternity, he did so with faith. I learned that while pilgrimage is hard, returning to the heart of God brings true restfulness. We may make and leave many homes, but our true home is where we invite God to abide in us.

Is an inner voice nudging you to slow down? Do you fear wondering if your life might fall apart if you rest and wait on God? He's looking for a dwelling place, sanctuaries and temples of complete yieldedness where He can make His home. Will you trust that as you empty your anxieties about the future at His feet, forsaking all your earthly homes for Him, that He will provide for all you need and come to make His home in you? Like Abraham, will you look beyond the visible? For our heavenly home, our godly inheritance, is the prize we can look forward to.

Whether you're struggling to let go of your securities to heed that still small voice or grappling with the shaking happening around you as an outcome of obeying God's call, know this: God, our master planner, has gone before you. All He requires of you is to enter the sacred space of rest in Him and wait expectantly on an eternal dwelling place that He has already prepared for you.

Friends, when we're willing to say goodbye to our earthly homes and look to our heavenly one, that's when we will truly find our greatest refuge—in God alone.

FOR REFLECTION

1. What does resting in God mean to you?
2. What about waiting on God has been most challenging for you?
3. How does knowing you have an eternal home in God change your perspective on your journey?

NEXT STEPS

1. Ask God how He wants you to rest. Then, in a chart like this one, write down practical ways you can practice more rest in your life and the adjustments you'll need to make in your schedule to make that happen.

Ways to practice more rest in my life:	Adjustments I'll need to make to accommodate more rest:

2. What are the costs of not entering into rest with God? List them.
3. On your calendar, schedule a day or more for a retreat with God. Plan a vacation, even.

PRAYER

God, I struggle with waiting on you and finding rest in you. Waiting requires an intentional slowing down, and that's hard for me. Will you enable me to enter into that sacred space of rest, to commune with you and hear your voice? I want to experience "extravagant wastefulness" in spending time with you. Today I choose to release all my self-striving and need for control to you and trust that even while I rest, you continue to work on my behalf. Amen.

20

offer God what you cherish most

> By faith Abraham, when he was tested, offered up Isaac, and he who had received the promises offered up his only begotten son, of whom it was said, "In Isaac your seed shall be called," concluding that God was able to raise him up, even from the dead, from which he also received him in a figurative sense.
>
> —Hebrews 11:17–19

WHEN I FIRST GOT THE EMAIL about this opportunity, my eyes glazed over. *Wanna go to Africa for six weeks?* It was from my professor at the national university, the same one who'd mistaken me as a cartoonist but eventually invited me into the COVID-19 outbreak response.

But then with a wry chuckle, I thought, *How ridiculous. I'm a mom to two toddlers now. Surely he knows that!* But inside, a flame flickered before going out. This was an opportunity I'd waited for all my adult life. The bold letters stared at me— WHO *Global Outbreak Alert Response Network Call for Humanitarian Assistance in Africa*. I emailed back, *Maybe if it was closer to home*. But internally I thought, *Sadly, this isn't for me. I'm sure God wants me to steward my children in this season.* Then I drank in my grief in a single sigh, and mourned this loss quietly alone. I clicked the email window shut.

Weeks later, while I was preparing to give a sermon titled "Will You Risk?" something in my spirit stirred. How could I preach about risk if I'd lost the willingness to risk? If I was a mother who claimed to model faith for her children, why did I justify my unavailability with my need to steward them?

That email, buried deep in my inbox, seemed to turn and lurch. I searched for it, and then one evening I showed it to Cliff for the first time.

"Of course you should say yes," he told me. "At least offer yourself, no?"

"Do you know what you're saying? What if I'm actually selected? I'd be away for at least six weeks." But I followed through, indicating my interest after all to the professor.

A week later, I left for my morning jog at dawn, a fresh email weighing heavy on my heart. I didn't want to break the news to Cliff, but as soon as I walked into our home, he saw my countenance and called me out. "The email came, didn't it? So where is it?"

"Congo," I said.

Silence.

The air froze like cracked glass.

"I need some time alone to process this," Cliff finally said.

I took the kids to the zoo, and when Cliff picked us up that afternoon, I saw that his eyes glistened with tears.

"I know people will ask me how I could possibly let you go to such a dangerous place," he said. "But God spoke to me today. How can I not let you go when the needs are so great and He's opened the door?"

Now tears glistened on both our faces.

Hebrews 11:17–19 says,

> By faith Abraham, when he was tested, offered up Isaac, and he who had received the promises offered up his only begotten son,

> of whom it was said, "In Isaac your seed shall be called," concluding that God was able to raise him up, even from the dead, from which he also received him in a figurative sense.

Abraham demonstrates unspeakable trust in God. After waiting for decades for his natural-born son, how could he lay a finger on him? While some speculate that Abraham knew God wouldn't follow through with the sacrifice, the words "concluding that God was able to raise him up" tells us that so great was his trust in God that he was willing to follow through with killing his son, believing that God Himself would resurrect him.

Through his obedience, Abraham's actions typified the love of the Father who did not spare His only begotten Son in order to fulfill His greater purposes. Abraham's offering of Isaac parallels God's offering of His Son, the ram parallels Christ's vicarious death, and Abraham's receiving Isaac alive typifies Christ's resurrection.[1] Because of Abraham's trust, we have a model of radical faith even when what is most precious to us is on the line. Even though Isaac was the answer to God's promises for Abraham's life, Abraham was willing to lay him down.

Perhaps the most difficult thing in our faith journeys is to lay at the altar what is most dear to us, especially when it doesn't make sense! Yet to make costly sacrifices in obedience to God even when we don't understand may be precisely what unlocks His purposes for our lives.

I hope the following story of my surrendering what was most precious to me in order to obey God's call will encourage you to believe that nothing is too dear a sacrifice to give to Him. Because when we obey, God Himself becomes our ultimate reward.

Give Up What You Treasure Most

The days that followed were an emotional roller coaster.

"The deployment to Congo isn't a good fit," came the email reply. My specialization was in health communication, and not being able to speak French in Congo was a major disadvantage. "We'll try to deploy you to a different place, but no guarantee."

No guarantee.

As I was scrolling through social media one Friday evening, I came across a quote and felt these fresh words drop into my spirit: "Make room for what you pray for." A physical sensation overcame me, and I knew it was the Holy Spirit inviting me to start putting my faith into action. Did I believe God was calling me? Just as in Genesis 22:3–6, when Abraham had to load his donkey, cut wood, prepare the knife and fire, and take his servants, was I willing to do what was necessary to start walking in faith—even if it hurt my heart to do so? I would have to leave my husband and young children behind.

As if in universal conspiracy, the next day my parents, who hadn't known a thing about my potential deployment, showed up with bags of my old belongings from their home. "You've left too many things at our place since you got married! Time to start taking them back!"

I opened the bags and was shocked. There before me lay all the clothes I'd packed for mission trips over the last decade. My African wear lay neatly folded in a stack in one of them. Of all the bags they chose to bring, they chose that one.

God was speaking.

I started packing.

Christmas came and went with no deployment news. I found myself smiling a big wide smile of relief inside. *Maybe they've forgotten me. Maybe there's no match. Maybe this was just a test of my faith and I passed. Great.*

The warning shot came right after Christmas. *Some countries have expressed interest in your deployment*, another email said. I felt God say, *Get ready*. But then no news again for days, and concern especially for my daughters persisted. When we told them about my willingness to go on a deployment mission alone, they protested vehemently—"No, Mama! No go!" I was their world, and my departure would be like the sun leaving its place in their universe, overturning their immutable laws of nature.

But over time, their protests gave way to curiosity. "Where is Africa, Mama? Are you taking a plane?" Even then my heart cringed with pain whenever I thought about leaving Sarah-Faith and Esther-Praise behind. *Give me grace, Lord,* I prayed when anxiety and guilt shook me awake in the wee hours of the morning.

At breakfast the next week, Sarah-Faith said, "Mama, before I slept last night, Jesus told me this." She took a deep breath and wagged her right index finger. "'Sarah-Faith, don't worry about your mummy when she's in Africa, because I will take care of her, okay?'"

Such is the childlike faith of a four-year-old. Such is the opportunity we have to impart faith by leaning on the One who gives us grace to ask for the faith we do not have.

When the email finally came, our hearts had made space for breaking news: *Urgent Request for Specialist deployment for COVID-19 Outbreak Response. You will be the first Singaporean doctor deployed in a joint partnership with UNICEF, GOARN, and the World Health Organization.*

Suddenly, I remembered a prophecy a pastor had shared with me four years earlier: "You will one day work with the United Nations to save lives." I scoffed back then. Me? The one who scraped through medical school? How could that be?

And then I remembered again what I'd written on my medical school application more than seventeen years earlier: "My hope is that someday I can partner with the United Nations and World Health Organization meaningfully to make an impact on our world." God did not forget that dream.

I sat back in awe and wonder at what God had done—through the seemingly long and winding path to Johns Hopkins, establishing Kitesong Global, being mistaken as a cartoonist. Everything seemed like a disparate series of events. Yet at every stage, God required faith. He required trust. He required an unbroken series of unwavering yeses for the fullness of the fruition of His dreams for my life. Only God Himself knew the intentionality of His divine sequence.

Do you struggle with believing God for His prophecies and promises to come to pass in your life? Does it feel like the events and situations you're currently a part of make no sense for where you need to go? Remember that your circumstances are central to your calling. God is mindful of where He has placed you. All He wants is your trust and unabashed yes.

One day while I was homeschooling, Sarah-Faith pointed to a picture she'd drawn in an exercise book. "Look, Mama. This is Papa, Meimei [little sis], and me on a plane with you. You are going to Africa, and Papa is taking us to have fun somewhere!" She beamed.

I'd been teaching my children a little rhyme I'd made up for them: *Even though we may be far apart, we are always joined heart to heart.* My daughter's plane drawing encapsulated the spirit of the rhyme. Though we would be in different geographical locations, we were in the same vehicle of faith, representing the same united mission. Jesus Himself was the pilot, directing us all.

"I will miss you, Mama," Sarah-Faith told me. "But God and Papa will take care of me and Meimei here in Singapore."

Once more, I teared. God was doling out His grace on me, saying, *I've got this.*

Your Sacrifice Is God's Greatest Gift

"Wow, that's a huge sacrifice you'll be making. You'll miss Chinese New Year [the largest festival celebrated by Singaporean Chinese], your own birthday, your firstborn's birthday, all told seven weeks of time with family. . . . That's too much of a loss, no?"

Waiting for the big announcement in the weeks ahead, with comments like the ones above, my heart hurt at the thought of leaving my family. The days were filled with dread.

Then that email came, and I had less than two weeks before leaving for the Kingdom of Eswatini in Africa. As I packed, I received a text message from a missions mobilizer that haunted me, *I do not recommend anyone leaving his or her spouse and children behind to do God's work.*

My eyes stung, once more smarting with hurt.

"You must go," Cliff said, affirming our decision. "God has given me much peace to release you. He will see our family through. Remember Sarah-Faith's plane drawing—even though we are geographically in different places, this is God's united mission for our whole family, to support you in this endeavor."

A month into my mission away from home, on the morning of my birthday, a pastor sent a voice message to me. "When we make sacrifices for God, He always comes back with a beautiful gift for us."

At once I thought of Abraham and Isaac. Abraham was intent on sacrificing his son to obey God. Yet God provided the ram in the thicket. His gift to Abraham was faith in His faithfulness and honor, the honor of forever being known as the patriarch of faith.

In Eswatini, the people greet one another with *Sawubona*, which means "I see you." It represents a seeing of one's soul, a gifting of one's presence to another, a recognition of a person's value and identity. As I learned the local language, I began to sense God Himself telling me, *Sawubona. I see you.*

Another pastor texted me one night. *This sacrifice you are giving to God is very costly, maybe more than you expected in terms of separation from your family. But it is a sweet savor unto the Lord. He is well aware.*

God spoke to me, *Sawubona, I see you. I see your sacrifice.*

It reminded me that as much as the Lord was watching Abraham's every move when He called him to sacrifice Isaac at the altar, He was watching—"seeing"—me too.

The local team said to me, "We spent many days asking God what Siswati name to give to you, Wai Jia. Names are very important here in Africa. God gave us a good name for you—Sibusissiwe." Used to describe someone who is a gift to others, it literally means "We are blessed because of you." Goose bumps came over me as I sensed the Holy Spirit speaking to me. *Because you have laid yourself on the altar as a sacrifice, God has turned you into a gift for others.*

Yet while they honored my being with them as a gift, I was gifted more than I'd ever imagined. One evening on the way back from visiting rural villages, I looked at a photo taken of me in my UNICEF vest, the Swazi *lihiya* (traditional wrap-skirt), holding my field notes, when the words of that pastor's prophecy now about eight years earlier came to life: "You will one day work with the United Nations to save the lives of millions of children."

A misfit in medical school, I'd scraped through every exam with my gut in my mouth, never knowing if I'd pass. I'd struggled with depression and an eating disorder. Even years after graduation, I'd watched my peers excel while I took a year off to serve in Uganda. People said I'd ruined my career. And the more I did medicine, the more I felt my life was a mistake.

But in that moment, on the cusp of turning a year older, God redefined my identity in Him, vocationally and intrinsically. I felt Him whisper, *This is who I made you to be. This is your birthday gift.*

My sacrifice became God's greatest gift back to me—the gift of identity.

As on my initial visit to Nepal, six weeks came and went. Before I left, as the local team threw a surprise farewell and tied a yellow traditional *lihiya* on me, I saw tears in people's eyes. I stood and said that although everyone had lamented what a costly sacrifice this deployment would be, God had showed me that when our sacrifice is done in obedience, what we'd perceived as loss turns into the biggest gift back to us.

Just before leaving Eswatini, I stared at a text I received in disbelief, my mouth open. My neighbor in Singapore, completely unaware that it was my final day in Africa, had sent me a photo of our flower bed in the community garden below our block. There in full bloom was the sunflower my girls had planted as a seed just before I'd left.

A warm sensation tingled up my arms. This was no coincidence but God's divine timing—and His way of reminding us, showing us, that what we'd sown in tears as a family, we now reaped with joy. Through the timely blossoming of our sunflower, God showed all of us His glorious fruit from our sacrifice, His visible glory from our invisible, inward growth.

Friends, if you're struggling to lay down something dear to you before God, remember this: no sacrifice for Him is too costly. For when we lay what is so dear to us at the altar, as Abraham did Isaac, God turns our tears to joy, our failings to breakthrough, and our losses into gifts. As we laid down our own family to obey God's call, a dream born seventeen years earlier and a prophecy given eight years earlier came to ultimate fruition.

Truly, we can trust "that all things work together for good to those who love God, to those who are the called according to His purpose" (Romans 8:28). There is no dream too small when we offer our all to Him. For all our sacrifices, we shall receive the greatest gift of all from God—knowing His Father's heart.

Following God Turns Ordinary Life Upside Down

When we follow God, ordinary life is turned upside down. Sacrifices become gifts. Loss turns to gain. Those who are last will be first (Matthew 20:16). Should it startle us, then, that glorifying God lies not in achieving our biggest dreams but in humbly yielding the smallest of our dreams for His purposes? While the world desires more hustling, God desires more waiting on Him—for it is in that sacred space of prayer and rest that God reveals His plans for our purposeful, fruitful work.

As I write the closing of this book, our family prepares to enter another season of fresh surrender as we pack up our lives in Singapore to relocate to Tanzania for missions long-term. The price feels costly, but we keep hearing His voice: *Dream brave, have faith.*

My prayer is that as you enter into quiet communion with God and allow Him to upend life as you know it, He will reveal to you that there is no dream too small or too big for Jesus when you give your all to Him. May He delight you with surprise as His Spirit buoys your kitedreams in the skies.

Keep dreaming brave.

FOR REFLECTION

1. What do you hold dear that's difficult for you to surrender?
2. When and how has God proven Himself faithful to you before, even in your sacrifice?
3. Have you ever experienced God turning your sacrifice into a gift? Describe that gift.

NEXT STEPS

1. Ask God what He desires for you to lay down. As you hear His voice, in a chart like this one, list those sacrifices in the first column.

My sacrifices to God:	God's gifts to me:

My sacrifices to God:	God's gifts to me:

2. Commit to filling the second column in the coming weeks or months as God reveals His gifts to you through your joyful surrender.
3. Meditate on the goodness of God and imagine your heart being filled with His love to overflowing. Praise Him aloud for that.

PRAYER

God, thank you for giving us the greatest sacrifice of all—Christ Himself. Because of that, no sacrifice is too big for me to surrender to you. I want to trust you like Abraham did and offer all I have to you. Will you take my dreams—big and small—and use them for your glory? Grant me unending trust and deepening faith as I offer my whole life to you. The opportunity to sacrifice my life is a gift in itself. Amen.

ACKNOWLEDGMENTS

WRITING THIS BOOK demanded that I dreamed brave, even when I doubted.

I wish I could tell you that I wrote *Dream Brave* in a single poetic breath. But I did not. The initial manuscript was written nine years ago, then refashioned from ashes, over and over. What you have in your hands was formed in the fire, a distillation of a God-led journey. Perhaps it is no coincidence that in rereading the words of my manuscript, I found courage to prepare our family for an epic adventure—a major move to Tanzania to serve vulnerable communities long-term, urging me to live out what I've written.

Initially when I pondered whether I should publish this book locally in Singapore or in the States, many urged me to take the easier, faster route. But weeks of prayer later, I dreamed of two trees, one taller than the other. I felt the Holy Spirit whisper to me, *Growing a bigger tree takes deeper faith, greater courage. Will you dream more bravely?*

So I dared to believe in the wilder dream.

But self-doubt assailed me. Why would an American publisher pick me, a little Singaporean woman with an Asian name no one can remember, and who doesn't speak English as her native language? Yet while writing the book, God steadied my shaky faith. Through the words He led me to write, He taught me to dream brave.

And now, through the words He's led me to polish and publish, He's leading our family to step out in faith into the mission field, for real.

There was no certainty that my hard work would come to fruition. I prayed this daily, *Lord, would you lead me to the publisher of your choice?* When editor David Sluka from Chosen Books picked me, I felt God smiling down, His eyes twinkling with good humor. Minutes after we met, as if to confirm His affirmation, the most beautiful rainbow appeared as a banner across the sky. Truly, this has been a far longer, more arduous journey than taking the local publishing route. But I have no regrets. Growing bigger dreams does take deeper faith and greater courage—but it is worth it.

To list all the people who have sowed into *Dream Brave* would be impossible, so to each and every one of you, *thank you.*

To my first editor Jennifer Edwards, for believing in me, for making a fledgling fly. Your tireless championing helped me keep writing when my hope wavered. You grew my faith and helped me find my voice.

To my agents Rachel Kent, Janet Grant, and the team at Books & Such Literary Management, for standing behind me every step of the way.

To editors David Sluka, Jean Bloom, and Bethany Lenderink, for taking a chance on me and cheering me on. To the rest of the team at Chosen Books, for bringing this book to life. To Dan Pitts, for the God-inspired book cover you created from my paintings—it is a special gift from God to me.

To every single social media follower and blog reader, to all my friends, for your sweet notes and sharing my work with the world. You have no idea how much your words of encouragement mean to me. What a privilege I have to journey in faith with you. What undeserved grace!

To those of you who have sowed sacrificially into our family, Kitedreams ministry, and Kitesong Global, you know who you are—I am indebted.

To my board members and team at Kitedreams and Kitesong Global, for journeying with me. To Pam, Tiffany, Marianne, Lydia, Dawn, Joy, and my growing team, for your unwavering faith, even when I felt unsure.

To Uncle Saba, Aunty Grace, Uncle Erick, Aunty Shanti, Eck Kheng, Aunty Anita, and Mr. Raymond James Ho, for changing my life. To Sarah Brogan, Susan Comiskey, and Juleen Shaw, for loving on me as spiritual mums, for spurring me on to hit the mark for my life.

To Pastor Yang Tuck Yoong and Pastor Lim Lip Yong, for speaking extraordinary faith into my life when I was most broken, for firing me up to push boundaries and giving me platforms to share my gifts with the world. To Cornerstone Community Church (Singapore), for your love and prayers.

To Pastor Hern Shung and Isaac Ong, for sowing time in my life discussing the Word and thus adding to the depth of this book. To Pastors Ben and Tricia, for turning my pain into hope.

To Heidi Baker, Bob Sorge, John Piper, Francis Chan, and the giants of faith, for your books written and bold lives lived that shaped so much of my faith.

To my very Asian parents, for raising me and taking the leap of faith to believe in my crazy dreams. To my in-laws, for being willing to have your hearts in your mouths as we embark on wild adventures. I am grateful for your stoic but steadfast support.

To my husband, Cliff, I learned most of the lessons in this book from God through your life of exemplary risk-taking and trust in Him. You have never stopped believing in me, even when I gave up on myself. You inspire me to take more radical risks for God every day. Sarah-Faith and Esther-Praise, you astound me daily with your enthusiastic, faith-filled prayers and wild courage. Every day I learn from the three of you how to dream brave. And to keep on doing so. You are my heroes of faith. How extraordinarily blessed I am that God chose me to be your wife and mama.

Let's dream brave together.

NOTES

Introduction

1. Kitedreams is the name of my ministry. See www.kitedreams.org.

Chapter 1 When Loved Ones Say No, Hold On to Faith

1. *Strong's Concordance*, s.v. "hupostasis," accessed on Bible Hub, https://biblehub.com/greek/5287.htm.

2. Aaron Berry, "What Does Jesus Mean by 'Faith as Small as a Mustard Seed,'" Crosswalk.com, May 26, 2020, crosswalk.com/faith/bible-study/what-does-jesus-mean-by-faith-as-small-as-a-mustard-seed.html.

3. "Verse 2, Matthew 17," in *Pulpit Commentary*, accessed on Bible Hub, https://biblehub.com/commentaries/pulpit/matthew/17.htm.

4. Matthew Everhard, "What Is Faith Like a Mustard Seed?" Logos, January, 2023, https://www.logos.com/grow/what-is-faith-like-a-mustard-seed/.

5. Everhard, "What Is Faith Like a Mustard Seed?"

Chapter 2 Say Yes to God—Again and Again

1. Robert Jamieson, A. R. Fausset, and David Brown, *Commentary Critical and Explanatory on the Whole Bible*, (Oak Harbor, WA: Logos Research Systems, Inc., 1997), 2:470.

2. See www.kitesong.com (USA) and www.kitesong.sg (Singapore).

3. Alexander Souter, *A Pocket Lexicon to the Greek New Testament* (Oxford, England: Clarendon Press, 1917), 271.

Chapter 3 Believe That Your Pain Has Purpose

1. Dr. Grant C. Richison, "Hebrews 11:12" on Verse-by-Verse Commentary, October 5, 2019, https://versebyversecommentary.com/2019/10/05/hebrews-1122/.

2. Richison, "Hebrews 11:12."

3. John Piper, "The Sale of Joseph and the Son of God," Desiring God, September 9, 2007, https://www.desiringgod.org/messages/the-sale-of-joseph-and-the-son-of-god.

Chapter 4 Hide in the Refuge of Prayer

1. "Hebrews 11:23," *Benson Commentary*, accessed on Bible Hub, https://biblehub.com/commentaries/hebrews/11-23.htm.

2. Henry T. Blackaby and Richard Blackaby, *Experiencing God*, revised and expanded (Nashville: B&H Publishing, 2008), 152.

Chapter 5 Give God Your All

1. "Hebrews 11:6," *Ellicott's Commentary for English Readers*, accessed on Bible Hub, https://biblehub.com/commentaries/hebrews/11-6.htm).

2. Josiah Ng, "The Wonderful Story of Cliff and Wai Jia," https://www.youtube.com/watch?v=jflEPT-oLCE&t=10s. This video was launched on our wedding day, and Josiah Ng is now an award-winning videographer. See www.youtube.com/@josiahng

Chapter 6 Make the More Excellent Sacrifice

1. Robert Jamieson, A. R. Fausset, and David Brown, *Commentary Critical and Explanatory on the Whole Bible* (1871), https://thirdmill.org/files/english/texts/jfb/JFB01.htm.

2. "Hebrews 11:4," *Pulpit Commentary*, accessed on Bible Hub, https://biblehub.com/commentaries/hebrews/11-4.htm.

3. "Hebrews 11:4," *Pulpit Commentary*, accessed on Bible Hub, https://biblehub.com/commentaries/hebrews/11-4.htm. "It is usual to find a reason in the nature of Abel's offering as signifying atonement, and to suppose his faith manifested in his recognition of the need of such atonement, signified to him, as has been further supposed, by Divine command."

Chapter 7 Persevere When Your Faith Is under Fire

1. Robert Jamieson, A. R. Fausset, and David Brown, *Commentary Critical and Explanatory on the Whole Bible*, (Oak Harbor, WA: Logos Research Systems, Inc., 1997), 2:474. See also, "Hebrews 11," *Matthew Poole's Commentary*, accessed on Bible Hub, https://biblehub.com/commentaries/poole/hebrews/11.htm.

Chapter 8 Wait on God and His Promises

1. John D. Barry, Douglas Mangum, Derek R. Brown, et al, "Hebrews 11:39–40" in *Faithlife Study Bible* (Bellingham, WA: Lexham Press, 2012, 2016).

Chapter 9 Take Risks by Faith

1. *Strong's Concordance*, s.v. "peira," accessed on Bible Hub, May 31, 2023, https://biblehub.com/greek/3984.htm.

2. Robert Jamieson, A. R. Fausset, and David Brown, *Commentary Critical and Explanatory on the Whole Bible*, (Oak Harbor, WA: Logos Research Systems, Inc., 1997), 2:474.

3. "Hebrews 11," *Matthew Poole's Commentary*, accessed on Bible Hub, May 31, 2023, https://biblehub.com/commentaries/poole/hebrews/11.htm.

4. Dr. Joel Hoomans, "35,000 Choices: The Great Choices of Strategic Leaders," The Leading Edge, March 20, 2015, https://go.roberts.edu/leadingedge/the-great-choices-of-strategic-leaders/.

5. John Piper, *Don't Waste Your Life* (Wheaton: Crossway Publishing, 2018), 74.

6. Piper, *Don't Waste Your Life*, 74.

Chapter 10 Fix Your Eyes on Greater Riches

1. Robert Jamieson, A. R. Fausset, and David Brown, *Commentary Critical and Explanatory on the Whole Bible*, (Oak Harbor, WA: Logos Research Systems, Inc., 1997), 2:473.

2. Jamieson, Fausset, Brown, *Commentary Critical and Explanatory on the Whole Bible*, 2:473.

3. "ὀνειδισμὸν," Bible Hub, https://www.biblehub.com/greek/oneidismon_3680.htm.

4. "ἀποβλέπω," Bible Hub, https://www.biblehub.com/greek/578.htm.

5. Dr. Henry Cloud and Dr. John Townsend, *Boundaries* (Grand Rapids, MI: Zondervan, 2017), 233.

Chapter 13 Build Your Ark of Faith

1. Robert Jamieson, A. R. Fausset, and David Brown, *Commentary Critical and Explanatory on the Whole Bible*, (Oak Harbor, WA: Logos Research Systems, Inc., 1997), 2:471.

2. Jamieson, Fausset, and Brown, *Commentary Critical and Explanatory on the Whole Bible*, 2:471.

3. "How Big Was Noah's Ark?" Ark Encounter, accessed June 5, 2023, https://arkencounter.com/noahs-ark/size/.

Chapter 14 Push Past Your Doubt

1. You can read commentaries about these two births and their significance on sites like https://biblehub.com/commentaries/genesis/16-12.htm.

2. "Hebrews 11:11," BibleRef, accessed June 6, 2023, https://www.bibleref.com/Hebrews/11/Hebrews-11-11.html.

3. The video she mentioned can be found can be found on YouTube entitled "The Wonderful Story of Cliff and Wai Jia" by Josiah Ng.

4. "First Stage of Labor," American Pregnancy Association, accessed June 6, 2023, https://americanpregnancy.org/healthy-pregnancy/labor-and-birth/first-stage-of-labor/.

5. "Understanding the Stages of Labor," Giving Birth Naturally, last modified June 6, 2023, https://www.givingbirthnaturally.com/stages-of-labor.html.

Chapter 15 Wrestle with God

1. "What Does Hebrews 11:21 Mean? " BibleRef, accessed June 8, 2023, https://www.bibleref.com/Hebrews/11/Hebrews-11-21.html.

2. Robert Jamieson, A. R. Fausset, and David Brown, *Commentary Critical and Explanatory on the Whole Bible*, (Oak Harbor, WA: Logos Research Systems, Inc., 1997), 2:473.

3. This video, titled "A Chance to Dream," can be found on Kitesong Global's YouTube channel, https://www.youtube.com/watch?v=CLVrktlhqLI&t=14s.

Chapter 19 Rest in God

1. Robert Jamieson, A. R. Fausset, and David Brown, *Commentary Critical and Explanatory on the Whole Bible*, (Oak Harbor, WA: Logos Research Systems, Inc., 1997), 2:472.

2. "Hebrews 11:10," BibleRef, accessed June 8, 2023, https://www.bibleref.com/Hebrews/11/Hebrews-11-10.html.

3. Shelly Miller, "Baby Steps," in *Rhythms of Rest* (Bloomington, MN: Bethany House Publishers, 2016).

4. Miller, *Rhythms of Rest*, 145.

Chapter 20 Offer God What You Cherish Most

1. Robert Jamieson, A. R. Fausset, and David Brown, *Commentary Critical and Explanatory on the Whole Bible*, (Oak Harbor, WA: Logos Research Systems, Inc., 1997), 2:473.

Wai Jia is an award-winning humanitarian doctor, keynote speaker, writer, and global health expert. She has consulted for international organizations such as the World Health Organization and UNICEF to amplify authentic connection with communities and impact people with better lives. She is a Risk Communication and Community Engagement (RCCE) specialist who equips communities with better health through data-driven health messaging.

Wai Jia is the founder of Kitesong Global, an international nonprofit that inspires youth to pursue their dreams and catalyze change among underserved communities. She is also the founder of Kitedreams, a Christian ministry that inspires people to dream bravely and live boldly.

Selected for *Forbes Asia*'s inaugural 30 under 30 list as a "disruptor reshaping the world," Wai Jia uses her edge in storytelling to cultivate creative strategies in health communication, bringing life-altering behavioral change to communities in need. Using the power of art and storytelling through her four self-illustrated picture books, she has raised over a million dollars for underserved women, children, and migrant workers around the world.

Having graduated from Johns Hopkins with a Master of Public Health with five awards and honors, she is also a Fulbright, Lee Kuan Yew, and Johns Hopkins scholar. She also holds a Master of Theological Studies from Zion Christian University (USA).

Wai Jia's more than sixteen years of speaking experience and life journey of adversity and strength, vulnerability, passion, and compassion make her a powerful and sought-after speaker in both faith-based and marketplace realms around the world, inspiring audiences to bravely pursue their dreams and live boldly with unabandoned fervor.

She is married to Cliff, and they have two young children. At the time of this book's release, their family is in the process of relocating to Tanzania to serve vulnerable communities.

Follow Wai Jia on Instagram @tamwaijia, www.kitedreams.org or on the Kitedreams Youtube channel (www.youtube.com/c/Kite dreams) to find inspirational resources that will speak faith and courage in lives for years to come.